E. Karkoschka
The Observer's Sky Atlas

E. Karkoschka

The Observer's Sky Atlas

With 50 Star Charts Covering the Entire Sky

Springer-Verlag
Berlin Heidleberg New York London Paris
Tokyo Hong Kong Barcelona Budapest

Erich Karkoschka

Nellingerstr. 45c, D-7000 Stuttgart 75, Fed. Rep. of Germany

With 50 star charts, 3 black and white photographs,
and 7 line drawings

Cover picture: Based on a photograph by the author it shows the southwest part of the constellation Sagittarius together with the brightest Milky Way clouds. North is to the upper left. The red nebula near the center is the Lagoon Nebula M8; the smaller cloud to the left of the picture is M24. Many other objects can be identified with the help of chart E20 (p. 93). The bright object on the left is the planet Mars.

Frontispiece: The sword of Orion, containing the Orion Nebula. Looking at it with a large telescope on a dark night gives one of the grandest views in the universe. The faint reflection nebula NGC 1973 lies half way to the top of the photograph, where the stellar group NGC 1981 can be seen.

Title of the original German editon: Atlas für Himmelsbeobachter
© Franckh'sche Verlagshandlung, W. Keller & Co., KOSMOS-Verlag, Stuttgart 1988

ISBN 3-540-51588-7 Springer-Verlag Berlin Heidelberg New York
ISBN 0-387-51588-7 Springer-Verlag New York Berlin Heidelberg

Library of Congress Cataloging-in-Publication Data. Karkoschka, Erich. [Atlas für Himmelsbeobachter. English] The observer's sky atlas : with 50 star charts covering the entire sky / Erich Karkoschka. p. cm. Translation of : Atlas für Himmelsbeobachter. ISBN 0-387-51588-7 (U.S.) 1. Astronomy–Atlases. 2. Stars–Atlases. I. Title. QB65.K3713 1990 523.8'022'3–dc20 89-26373

9 8 7 6 5 4 3 2

Printed on acid-free paper

Contents

Star Charts and Catalog

Explanatory Notes

Index of Figures and Tables

Tables

Explanatory Notes

Introduction

Can you remember being impressed by a clear starry sky? Look at the Milky Way through binoculars and it will reveal its many hundreds of thousands of stars, double stars, stellar clusters, and nebulae. If you are a new observer, it is not that easy to find your way in this swarm of stars, but this atlas tries to make it as easy as possible. So now it is not just experienced amateurs that can enjoy looking at the heavens.

Two additional observing aids are recommended. The first is a planisphere, where one can dial in the time and day in order to see which constellations are visible and where they are in the sky. The second is an astronomical yearbook. It lists the current positions of the planets and all important phenomena.

So, let us begin our journey around the night sky, and see what the universe can reveal to us!

Facing page, top: The constellation Cygnus (Swan) in the midst of the northern Milky Way. The photograph gives an impression of the uncountable stars in our Milky Way. This becomes more conspicuous when you sweep through Cygnus with binoculars. Under a very dark sky, one can try to find the North America Nebula, Pelican Nebula, and Veil Nebula (see p. 47). These are difficult nebulae and are only barely visible on this photograph as well. For orientation: Deneb is the bright star on the left side; Albireo is near the right edge, nearly as high as Deneb

Facing page, bottom: The region around the constellation Crux (Southern Cross) in the southern Milky Way. Aside from the Magellanic Clouds, this part is a special attraction of the southern sky. Directly to the lower left of the cross is a dark nebula, the Coalsack. It displays beautiful detail in binoculars. In the right part of the photograph is the bright Eta Carinae Nebula, surrounded by bright clusters. The star Eta Carinae illuminates the nebula and is currently not visible to the naked eye, although it was the second brightest star in the sky during two decades of the nineteenth century. It is a candidate for the next supernova explosion in our part of the Milky Way. The enormous flash of the explosion might already be on its 6000-year journey to us

Sky Atlases

Most sky atlases can be classified into one of two major groups according to the number of stars they contain. Some atlases only show the stars visible to the naked eye. As there are not more than a few thousand such stars, such charts can be simple and clear and can be arranged in a handy format. They are ideal for all naked-eye observations. The other group of atlases contains the stars visible through binoculars or telescopes. As there are a million stars within the reach of binoculars, such atlases need hundreds of charts, often arranged in several volumes. They are ideal for observations with binoculars and telescopes.

This atlas steers a middle course. It contains the whole sky visible to the unaided eye (limiting magnitude 6^m), and finder charts for 250 interesting objects for binoculars and small telescopes (limiting magnitude 9^m). Since these finder charts only cover approximately ten percent of the whole sky, it was possible to put all this information into a very convenient format.

Some atlases contain as many codes and labels as possible for each object. They are quite useful for work at home at the desk. The other extreme is represented by photographic atlases containing no labels at all. They are recommended when it comes to comparison with the real sky. This atlas again lies between the two extremes. The star charts are clear and contain just one label for important objects, since all the other data can always be found on the page facing the chart.

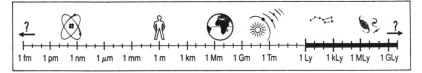

Figure 1: Between the size of an atomic nucleus and the furthest known objects in the universe, we have explored 41 orders of magnitude. This atlas contains objects further than one light-year: that means the last ten orders of magnitude. Nobody can really imagine these distances. But if we shift these ten orders of magnitude to the left, to the sizes we feel comfortable with, then we can get at least a feel for the world of stars and galaxies

Catalogs

As well as a naked-eye atlas and a binocular atlas, observers also use a catalog to look up important data such as double-star separations or the magnitudes of nebulae. This atlas combines these three functions. To work with different books can be troublesome because, between them, object selection and labeling may be quite different. In this atlas all objects labeled in the charts are listed in the tables on the facing page, naturally with the same designation, and all objects in the tables are labeled in the facing star charts. This makes observing as easy as possible.

Catalogs for scientific analysis need to contain original, unbiased measurements, even if some measurements represent impossible values such as negative parallaxes. On the other hand, the values given in this book are based on several sources and thereby represent the best estimation possible with today's knowledge. The major sources are: *Sky Catalogue 2000.0*, the *Yale Bright Star Catalogue*, the *Smithsonian Astrophysical Observatory* (SAO) *Star Catalog, 291 Doppelsternephemeriden für die Jahre 1975–2000, Ovschni Katalog Peremenich Zvjezd, Synopsis der Nomenklatur der Fixsterne, Délimitation Scientifique des Constellations, Burnham's Celestial Handbook*, and the *Webb Society Deep-Sky Observer's Handbook*.

As there are no more than some thousand sets of data, it was possible to compare each entry with different sources. Where there were great discrepancies, the author's observations were also considered. For example, the combined magnitude of the binary Algieba is listed in 14 different sources 8 times as $1^m.8$–$1^m.9$ and 6 times as $2^m.1$–$2^m.3$. Even in a city with artificial lights, a naked-eye observer can estimate its magnitude to better than half a magnitude.

Often it is not that easy to separate right and wrong. This is especially true for all information concerning distance. Most distances of stars further away than 100 light-years can only be estimated from the stars' spectra, where small uncertainties can easily change the distance by a factor of 2–3. An extreme example is the Quasar 3C 273. Today's most plausible assumption for its large red shift is the expansion of the universe. Then 3C 273 must be at a cosmological distance of about 2000 million light-years. On the other hand, direct measurements of its parallax can only exclude distances less than 500 light-years. There is an

Table 1: Small conversion table between light-years and parsecs. All distances are given in light-years in this atlas, while professional astronomers prefer the parsec as a unit of distance. 1 light-year = 9.46×10^{12} kilometers = 5.88×10^{12} miles. 1 parsec = 3.26 light-years. Distances in the range of this table are rounded to the nearest unit. The rounding error is much smaller than uncertainties in the distances

light-years (ly)	100	120	150	200	250	300	400	500	600	800	1000
parsecs (pc)	30	36	45	60	75	90	120	150	180	240	300

uncertainty by a factor of several million! It is wise to be extremely cautious when interpreting astronomical data!

Object Selection

This atlas contains 250 nonstellar objects listed under the general term "nebula": planetary nebulae, diffuse nebulae, open or galactic star clusters, globular star clusters, and galaxies. In addition to all 110 Messier objects, 140 additional nebulae that have magnitudes like those of many Messier objects have been selected. Among similar nebulae, those further north were slightly favored in the selection. All these nebulae can be observed with an amateur's telescope. Following each table of nebulae is a short description of each object for binoculars or an amateur's telescope under good sky conditions. Here the term "amateur's telescope" is considered to be a telescope with an aperture lying in the range 60–200mm (2.4–8 in.). Today, many amateurs own still larger telescopes. This atlas is also useful for them, but it only satisfies part of their telescopes' capabilities.

The catalog of stars contains 900 naked-eye stars. It is complete up to magnitude 4^m0. There are 561 stars up to this magnitude. Most of the fainter listed stars are doubles or variables.

Many thousands of double and multiple stars are observable with amateurs' telescopes. 250 interesting ones are listed in the table of binaries. Their components are at least 8^m0, their combined light brighter than 6^m0. Apart from a few very close binaries, all these can be separated in an amateur's telescope.

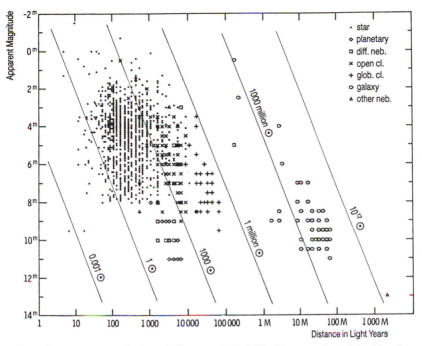

Figure 2: Apparent magnitude and distance of all 1423 objects catalogued in this atlas; binary components are indicated individually. Horizontal and vertical alignments are artifacts of rounding. The steep lines show the luminosity relative to the solar luminosity (if interstellar absorption is neglected)

The tables also list data for 80 variable stars visible to the naked eye. Variable stars with a variation of at least a quarter of a magnitude were considered. All those which get brighter than fifth magnitude (and a few fainter ones) are included.

Celestial Coordinates

In astronomy, many different coordinate systems are commonly used. To enjoy the night sky it is not necessary to tangle with the mathematics of coordinates. However, it is quite useful to become familiar with the most important coordinate system, the celestial equatorial system. One can

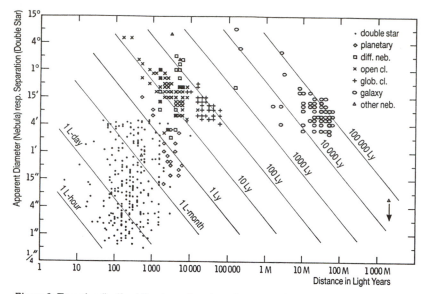

Figure 3: True size (inclined lines) as a function of apparent size and distance. The true size refers to the extent perpendicular to the line of sight. The radial extent is unknown for most objects. One light-hour is approximately 1000 million kilometers or seven astronomical units (AU)

imagine the equatorial system as a projection of the earth's longitude and latitude circles from the center of the earth onto the celestial sphere. Right ascension corresponds to geographical longitude; declination corresponds to geographical latitude. In the same way that Greenwich marks the zero meridian on earth, the first point of Aries serves as the zero point for the right ascension: it is the location of the sun on March 20/21. From there, right ascension is measured towards the east from 0° to 360°, or, more often, from 0^h to 24^h (hours) with $1^h = 15°$. Declination increases as geographical latitude from 0° at the equator to 90° at the poles. Northern declinations are positive, southern ones negative. The position of a star is uniquely determined by its right ascension and declination.

Precession

Since the first point of Aries slowly moves across the constellations, the coordinates of the stars are constantly changing. The coordinates in this atlas are accurate in the year 2000 (epoch 2000.0). Within 10 years the change of coordinates is less than $9' = 0.15°$, so in the period 1990–2010 the given coordinates can be used for most practical purposes without applying any correction.

Sidereal Time

The starry sky and the celestial coordinate system complete one revolution every day. Stars at the same declination describe the same orbit on the celestial sphere. After one sidereal day of 23^h56^m, every star is back at its original position. The sidereal time indicates the rotation since the first point of Aries passed the meridian. The meridian stretches from south to north, passing through the zenith. All stars reach their highest point on the meridian. At 0^h00^m sidereal time the first point of Aries is on the meridian. At 1^h sidereal time stars with the right ascension 1^h are passing across the meridian, and so on. Knowing the current sidereal time defines the region of the sky which is visible best. The current sidereal time can be estimated easily with the table on p. 121.

Arrangement of Star Charts

In this atlas the whole sky is divided into 48 regions which are grouped into three sections: N = northern sky, E = equator and ecliptic, S = southern sky. The northern sky here means the area north of about $30°$ declination. From mid-northern latitudes, for example, it is clearly visible every night. The very first chart (NP = north polar region) contains stellar magnitudes to 13^m for estimating the limiting magnitude to the unaided eye, binoculars, and telescopes. The section for the equator and ecliptic contains declination zones where the sun, moon, and planets have their paths. Constellations in this region are only visible at certain times. Of course, they are best visible near the meridian. The sky south of $-36°$ declination is labeled here as the southern sky. It cannot be observed north of 50° latitude. But further south more and more of the southern sky becomes visible. Northern-hemisphere observers should not miss the opportunity to observe the beauties of the southern sky when traveling south.

Within each of the three groups the charts are ordered in right ascension from 0 to 24. For example, the charts N 12, E 12, and S 12 all display regions near 12^h right ascension. The objects in the tables are also ordered in right ascension, which increases from right to left in the charts. Furthermore, the even-numbered charts E 0, E 2, ... mostly contain regions south of the equator, while E 1, E 3, ... display regions mostly north of the equator. To find a particular chart quickly, consult the key charts at the end of the book.

Directions in the Sky

On the earth we are very familiar with the direction of the four cardinal points. In the same way, directions are defined at each point in the sky. North is the direction to the celestial north pole near Polaris. West is the direction in which the sky is carried by the diurnal rotation of our planet. Therefore west is sometimes called preceding, and east is called following. When looking up at a constellation lying in the south, north is up, west is right, south is down, and east is left. We note that east and west on star charts are opposite to east and west on maps. However, in common with maps, all charts in this atlas have north at their top.

When comparing a chart with the sky it is important to know the directions in the sky in order to turn the charts until they match the sky. For comparison with rising constellations, the charts need to be turned somewhat counterclockwise, and clockwise for setting constellations. In an inverting telescope, directions are particularly important, even if they are not so clear. If you are not sure of them, just watch the motion of the stars through the eyepiece (clock drive off). They always move to the west. Further, notice that a standard diagonal gives a mirror image (if the total number of reflections is odd). You would need to look through a mirror at the charts in order to match the view in the eyepiece. Therefore the use of a diagonal is not recommended for deep-sky-object hunting.

Double-star observers often want to know the exact direction of a companion from the primary star. This is specified by the position angle,

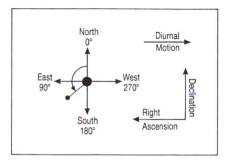

Figure 4: Directions on the celestial sphere and position angle of double stars

measured from north (0°) towards east (90°), south (180°), and west (270°); see also Fig. 4. For example, a position angle of 135° indicates that the fainter component is southeast of the brighter one.

Size and Scale

Distance and size in the sky are measured in degrees, arc minutes, and arc seconds (1°= 60', 1' = 60"). In this atlas, declination is given in degrees, the size of nebulae in arc minutes, and the separation of double stars in arc seconds. There are no mixed entries like 8°48' or 3'12". This latter practice is continuing to disappear from astronomical tables.

When using star charts it is important to have an idea about the scale of the charts. The star charts in this atlas have a scale of 4.5°/cm (11.5°/in.), the round enlarged sections 1.1°/cm (2.8°/in.). Distances in the sky can be quite accurately estimated with your hand. If you hold it about 60 cm from your eye, 1cm on your hand corresponds to 1° in the sky. Once you have measured some sizes on your hand, you will always have a "handy" aid present at your observation sessions.

When observing with binoculars and telescopes it is very helpful to know the diameter of the field of view. You can estimate this by comparing it with the disk of the full moon, which is about 30' = 0.5° across. Better still are data from the manufacturer, or your own measurements. For example, a field of 5° in binoculars corresponds to a 4.5 cm (1.8 in.) circle in the round enlarged sections of this atlas. Trying to work with star charts can be difficult for the inexperienced observer, but it becomes easy by knowing direction and scale.

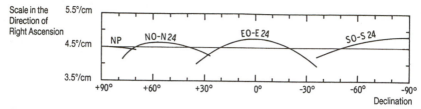

Figure 5: The scale of the star charts in the east–west direction. The scale in the perpendicular direction (in declination) is 4.5°/cm everywhere. The difference between both scales is small; the charts are nearly undistorted

All maps and charts are somewhat distorted, because the sky is spherical and charts are flat. Therefore the scale is not constant. Star charts containing a large fraction of the whole sky (e.g. p. 130) necessarily have large distortions. For all other charts the distortion is kept low by using appropriate projections. These projections show all right-ascension circles as straight lines, perpendicularly intersecting the declination circles throughout. The scale in the direction north–south (declination) is exactly 4.5°/cm (11.5°/in.), while the scale in the direction east–west varies a little around this value as shown in Fig. 5. The round enlarged sections are stereographic projections and are practically free of distortion because of the small area of sky shown.

Magnitude

Brightness in astronomy is measured in (stellar) magnitudes, denoted by a superscript [m]. The unaided eye can see stars to approximately 6^m, depending on sky conditions. Binoculars and telescopes reach to much fainter stars (see Table 2). The star charts in this atlas represent the naked-eye view (limiting magnitude 6^m), while the round enlarged sections match the view in small binoculars and in a finder (limiting magnitude 9^m).

Magnitudes of stars can be measured very accurately. They are given here to an accuracy of $0^m.1$ (pronounced "point-one em"). On the other hand, nebulae do not have a well-defined circumference. Thus their magnitude is very dependent on the area regarded as part of the nebula. It is not surprising that the magnitude of a nebula varies by one or two magnitudes in different sources. Therefore nebular magnitudes are given here

Table 2: Limiting magnitude and resolution under good conditions (dark sky, steady air, high in the sky, good optics). For nebulae one should decrease the limiting magnitude by one. The right side of the table gives the number of visible nebulae and double stars in this atlas. The visibility of each object is marked in the column "Vis." in the tables p. 24 ff. The given visibility is for testing purposes. Less-determined observers should look for easier objects

Vis.	Observing Instrument	Magni- fication	Aperture		Limit. Mag.	Reso- lution	Ne- bulae	Bi- naries
ey	unaided eye	$1\times$	5 mm	0.2 in.	6^m	$300''$	39	-
Ey	very good eye	$1\times$	8 mm	0.3 in.	7^m	$200''$	57	5
op	small opera glasses	$2\times$	15 mm	0.6 in.	8^m	$150''$	110	17
Op	large opera glasses	$4\times$	25 mm	1.0 in.	9^m	$80''$	147	37
bn	small binoculars	$8\times$	40 mm	1.6 in.	10^m	$40''$	191	58
Bn	large binoculars	$15\times$	60 mm	2.4 in.	11^m	$20''$	238	95
tl	small telescope	$20-200\times$	80 mm	3.2 in.	12^m	$1.''5$	249	205
Tl	large telescope	$35-350\times$	150 mm	6.0 in.	13^m	$0.''8$	250	245

to half magnitudes as was done in the *New General Catalogue* (NGC) one hundred years ago (magnitudes are rounded to whole magnitudes for planetary and diffuse nebulae). The size and magnitude of a nebula refer in this atlas to what can be seen under a very dark sky. Under less-favorable conditions nebulae will appear fainter and smaller, while professional equipment can trace them further out.

When you actually observe nebulae, the total magnitude is often not as important as the surface brightness or brightness density. (Both the total magnitude and the surface brightness are listed in the tables under "Mag.".) The surface brightness refers to an area of a $5'$ circle ($5' = $ resolution of unaided eye). Nebulae with a high surface brightness (5–7^m) allow a high magnification. Thus they can be observed in moonlight or artificial-light pollution. Fainter objects (8–10^m) require a low power and a dark sky. To find nebulae with a still fainter surface brightness (11–12^m) is a challenge, sometimes even to experienced observers. The surface brightness might vary across the nebula, so that bright stars in a cluster or a galaxy core can be more easily observed, while the outer nebular regions might be much more difficult to see. Although knowledge of the surface brightness is very valuable for the deep-sky observer, it is not listed in other atlases or catalogs.

Resolution

The eye has a resolution of $5' = 300''$: it can resolve double stars of $5'$ separation or more. Very good eyes can resolve closer binaries, like ε Lyrae, of $3.5'$ separation. Double stars with a very faint companion are more difficult. When observing with binoculars and telescopes, the resolution increases to $300''$/power, assuming perfect optics, although the resolution is also limited by the aperture and is in the best case $120''$/aperture in mm ($5''$/aperture in in.). The resolution of the eye and the telescope match each other if the magnification is 2.5 times the aperture in mm ($60 \times$ aperture in in.). This is the highest efficient power. It can be used for binaries under good conditions. On the other hand, most nebulae require a much lower power.

Unfortunately, most standardly equipped telescopes come with high, and completely useless, magnifications, while the so-important low powers, with large fields of view, are missing. A long focal-length eyepiece can easily close this gap. The useful standard magnification is about ten times lower than the highest efficient magnification, that is aperture/4 ($6 \times$ aperture in in.). Many binoculars are optimal in this respect and easier to use than a telescope where such a magnification is missing. Many manufacturers like to save money on another part of the telescope as well: the finder. Many finders are made for long searching rather than quick finding. A good finder should have at least a 50mm aperture and a $5°$ field of view. The purchase of a good finder can change frustrating finding into exciting observing. Note also that observing with binoculars is much more enjoyable if they are mounted on a tripod.

Designations

There are many types of designation for astronomical objects. For the observer it is sufficient to be familiar with just the most important ones. Constellations are designated by their 88 official Latin names. Abbreviations for, and meanings of, the constellations are listed on pp. 128,129. Bright stars are designated by the Bayer Greek letter and/or Flamsteed number, with the constellation name in the genitive, for example α Ori = alpha Orionis = 58 Orionis. Latin letters are used for variables and stars without a Bayer or Flamsteed designation. Comments in the tables indicate if a designation is less commonly used. Some stars also have names which are mostly spelled here according to their original form. Today their spelling varies in different languages. Names are not that useful for the identification of stars, except the most common ones which are printed bold in the tables. The pronunciation of these foreign names poses problems for many people who are not familiar with Latin, Greek, and Arabic. For simplicity the names are often pronounced just as if they were English. Actually, the original pronunciation is much simpler than today's English, since every letter is always used in the same way: a as [ah], e as [eh], i as [ee], u as [oo], c as [k], etc. ξ Cep is pronounced [ksee keh-feh-ee]. Of course, there is no right and wrong in pronunciation, just as a dialect is not a right or a wrong language.

In the eighteenth century, Messier catalogued 103 nebulae which were later extended to 110 objects. In a few cases his description is not clear, so that some people disagree with the generally accepted identification. Messier objects are designated by an "M". A much more complete list of nonstellar objects is the *New General Catalogue* (NGC) with the *Index Catalogue* (IC). NGC objects are labeled by the number alone, while *Index Catalogue* objects start with "IC". All the nebulae in this atlas are listed on p. 124.

Spectral Type

From the spectrum of a star, astronomers can derive the surface temperature, chemical composition, size, mass, and rotation of the star. These are important quantities for the professional astronomer. For the observer, the color of a star is most interesting. Stars are classified according to their spectrum into spectral type and luminosity class. Spectral types are O, B, A, F, G, K, M, C, each group subdivided into tenths by a number 0–9. O stars are the hottest and bluest ones, C stars are the coolest and reddest ones. The true luminosity of a star is indicated by its luminosity class. Luminosity classes are Ia, Ib, II, III, IV, V, with Ia containing the most luminous stars, called supergiants, and V marking the main sequence. Current equipment makes it possible to subdivide classes and add special types which we will not consider in this book.

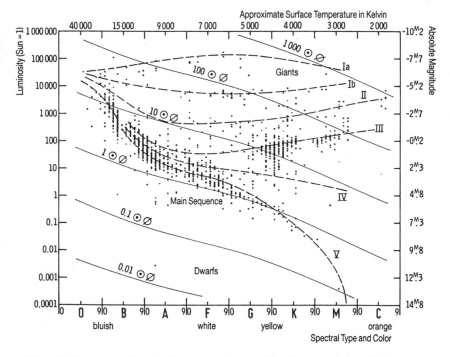

Figure 6: Hertzsprung–Russell diagram, supplemented by the spectral class C. Most stars seem to be more luminous than our sun, but this is only a selection effect. Actually, more than 80 percent of the stars are less luminous than our sun. Dashed lines indicate the approximate location of the luminosity classes. Uninterrupted lines indicate stellar diameters in units of the solar diameter (1.4 million km = 865 000 miles). The absolute magnitude is the magnitude seen from a distance of 10 pc = 32.6 light-years

A spectral type starting with a "d" means that the spectrum is a composite of the two spectra of a double star. Spectral types for each component are listed in the tables of binaries. Beautiful color contrast is indicated by a "!" between both spectral types. To be accurate it should be mentioned that the spectral type is not completely correlated with the color of a star, and that stars further than about 1000 light-years appear redder because of interstellar absorption.

Astronomers determine spectral types by the absorption lines in the spectrum of a star. The luminosity can be derived from the magnitude of the star if its distance is known. Plotting luminosity versus spectral type gives the Hertzsprung–Russell diagram (see Fig. 6). M stars are often referred to as deeply red stars, because they are near the red end of the diagram. By no means does this indicate that M stars emit deeply red light. Actually, they are whiter than what is called white heat. A bright M star in a telescope can be well compared to a small, unfiltered flashlight bulb. Both shine somewhat yellow, but certainly not red. (Incidentally, the observer is recommended to use a deeply red-filtered flashlight for deep-sky observations. After using a white light the eye needs 30 minutes to reach maximum sensitivity again. A faint red light does not influence the adaptation of the eye).

Double Stars

There are two groups of double stars or binaries: intrinsic binaries and optical binaries. They are intrinsic if the stars are close to each other in space. They are optical if they are along our line of sight but at different distances. In many cases it is not known if a double star is an intrinsic or optical one. In this atlas we use a purely observational criterion for selecting binaries. If the separation between two stars is more than $5' = 300''$ they appear as two stars in the table of stars. If they are closer than $300''$ the table of stars only contains one star with the combined light of the components, while the table of binaries lists them individually. Since $5'$ is the resolution of the naked eye, the table of stars gives the stars as they appear to the unaided eye. The table of binaries shows the telescopic view.

Table 3: The separation of double stars and the nebula size, which is magnified to the apparent size of 5′ (limit of resolution), to full-moon size, and to the size of the full field of view

magnification	1×	3×	6×	15×	30×	60×	150×	300×
limit of resolution	5′	100″	50″	20″	10″	5″	2″	1″
appears full-moon size	0.5°	10′	5′	2′	1′	0.5′	0.2′	0.1′
fills field of view	50°	1000′	500′	200′	100′	50′	20′	10′

Binaries which do not display a significant relative motion between 1990 and 2010 have only one entry in the columns of position angle and separation. For faster-moving binaries several rows are given, one for 1990 and further ones until 2010. To be exact, the position angle and separation refer to the beginning of a given year, but this really only matters for the fastest binaries.

For multiple stars, further components are listed below the companion. The position angle and separation are measured from the primary star for all companions, except if it is indicated by a "C" that they are measured from the companion directly listed above.

Variable Stars

There are two main groups of variables: eclipsing binaries (two stars occult each other) and intrinsic variables (physically changing stars). Eclipsing binaries can be divided into Algol-type and β Lyrae-type stars. Algol-type variables shine mostly at constant, maximum light. Their brightness drops steeply when the stars are eclipsing each other. β Lyrae stars constantly change their brightness. The two stars are so close that they are elongated by gravitational interaction. Sometimes we look at their narrow side, sometimes at their wide side. Intrinsic variables are divided into irregular, semiregular, δ Cephei-type stars or Cepheids (short period), and Mira-type stars (long period), and novae which are not listed in this atlas. This is still only a rough classification: there are more than 50 subtypes of variable stars.

For variable-star observers, the tables list important information. The time of a maximum or minimum (usually the first one in 1990) is listed

Table 4: Classification of variable stars

Intrinsic Variable Stars	
irregular ⎫ semiregular ⎭	giant and supergiant pulsating stars
Mira type	long period, small variations in period, large amplitude
Cepheid	short period, quite regular, named after δ Cephei
Eclipsing Binaries	
Algol type	short minima, long constant maximum light, very regular
β Lyrae type	constantly varying, very regular

as the Julian Date under "Max." or "Min.". The Julian Date for the beginning of each month is listed on p. 122. Further maxima and minima can be easily calculated by adding a multiple of the given period. Observers also like to know the shape of the light variation between two maxima or minima, called the light curve, as a function of phase. The phase is the time since the last maximum (for intrinsic variables) or minimum (for eclipsing binaries), expressed as a fraction of the period. It goes from zero to one within one period. If the minimum of an intrinsic variable occurs later than phase 0.5, the brightness decrease is slower then the brightness increase. An example for calculating the phase makes it clear: What was the magnitude of Algol during the total lunar eclipse on February 9, 1990 at $19^h 12^m$ UT? According to the table on p. 122 and the formula on p. 123, this date is Julian Date 2447932.30. Algol's data are, according to p. 30: period 2.86731 days, minimum 2447895.22, maximum light during phase 0.07–0.93. Now we calculate (2447932.30 − 2447895.22)/2.86731 = 12.93. This indicates that 12 complete periods occurred since the first minimum in 1990, and that the phase in the current period is 0.93. Since maximum light lasts just until phase 0.93, Algol started its decline towards its minimum exactly at that time. It reached the minimum 0.07 periods, or almost 5 hours, later.

Eclipsing binaries also display a secondary minimum centered between two primary minima (at phase 0.5). But this cannot be clearly recognized for most variables since it is too shallow.

The given magnitude range for variables in the table of stars refers to extreme magnitudes. Some variables do not go to their extremes in each period. Mira can reach magnitude $2^m 0$, but at other maxima only $4^m 0$. The entry "Mean" then indicates the mean magnitude or mean-magnitude range within one period.

Nebulae

Most nebulae belong to one of the five groups of planetaries, diffuse nebulae, open and globular star clusters, and galaxies.

Planetary nebulae: These are called "planetaries" because in a telescope they look like small, greenish disks, just like Uranus. They are gaseous nebulae and consist of the outermost shell of a hot central star, blown into space many thousands of years ago. Most planetaries appear stellar in binoculars. Only at high power do they reveal their shapes. Rings and disks are the most common shapes. Planetary nebulae are more conspicuous through a green filter, or rather a nebular filter. This

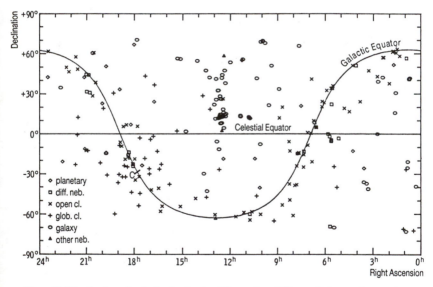

Figure 7: Distribution of nebulae in the sky. Planetaries, diffuse nebulae, and open clusters lie near the central plane of the Milky Way, the galactic equator. Globular clusters are also found far away from this plane, but are concentrated toward the center C of the Milky Way. Galaxies avoid the galactic equator and are densest in the Virgo Cluster (near center of figure). In the plane of the Milky Way, interstellar absorption by dust limits the visibility to approximately 10 000 light-years. Looking out of the plane, we have a clear view millions of light-years deep into the universe. Similarly, on a hazy day, the visibility towards the horizon may be very limited, yet the sun, some 150 million kilometers away, can be seen clearly high up in the sky

Table 5: Classification of nebulae. Abbreviations listed under "Type" and "Shape" are used in the table of nebulae

Type	Shape	Description	Type	Shape	Description
Plan		PLANETARY	Glob		GLOBULAR CLUSTER
	R	ring shaped		I	very distinct core
	D	disk shaped		.....	.....
	A	anomalous, irregular		.....	.....
	0–9	oblateness		XII	very smooth central area
Diff		DIFFUSE NEBULA	Galx		GALAXY
	Em	emission nebula		E	elliptical galaxy
	Re	reflection nebula		L	lenticular, S0 galaxy
	Fi	filamentary supernova rem-		S	spiral galaxy with:
	0–9	oblateness nant		a	large core, short arms
				b	medium core, spiral arms
Open		OPEN STAR CLUSTER		c	small core, long arms
	r	rich in stars		d	no core, very long arms
	m	medium number of stars		m	irregular spiral arms
	p	poor in stars		Ir	irregular galaxy
	n	associated nebulosity		0–9	oblateness
oblateness = 10 × (major diameter − minor diameter) / major diameter						
0 = circular ..... 9 = extremely elongated						

transmits the green light of the nebula, but absorbs most of the other parts of the spectrum, thereby increasing the contrast between nebula and background. The colors of nebulae are barely visible in amateurs' telescopes. But in very large telescopes planetaries shine intensely green or bluish-green. It is curious that planetaries show up red on most photographs. Color film is suited for reflected sunlight or incandescent light. The spectrum of emission nebulae like planetaries is so different that normal film is not able to record them in true color. Of course, when one is aware of this effect, it does not decrease the value of astrophotography.

Diffuse nebulae: These consist of gas and dust. Usually one finds them within a young open cluster where new stars are forming from their gas and dust. They are called emission nebulae if most of the light is gaseous emission. Their color, and the use of nebular filters, is the same as for planetaries. Filamentary supernova remnants also emit a similar spectrum. They do not tell the story of the birth of stars, but rather of the end of a star's life. Diffuse nebulae are called reflection nebulae if most of the light is reflected or scattered light from a star by interstellar dust. They are more difficult to observe since their contrast cannot be enhanced by the use of nebular filters.

Open star clusters: Open clusters might appear nebulous to the naked eye or in small binoculars. But in a telescope they are always resolved into individual stars. Many open clusters are very young compared to our solar system. Gas and dust forming new stars are often associated with them. Rich open clusters consist of more than a hundred stars. Clusters poor in stars (less than 50 stars) are usually inconspicuous.

Globular star clusters: Globular clusters are so distant that individual stars only become visible in telescopes. In binoculars, and partially in small telescopes, the hundreds of thousands of stars appear as a nearly circular glow, more or less condensed towards the center. While open clusters are only several million years old, globular clusters are among the oldest objects in our universe. Some determinations put them at an age of almost 25 000 million years. On the other hand, the universe cannot be much older than 10 000 million years according to some measurements of its expansion. Again, one has to be cautious when interpreting astronomical data.

Galaxies: These are systems of stars like our own Milky Way. Large telescopes reveal their different shapes. Elliptical galaxies appear as a featureless, elliptical glow. Lenticular galaxies look similar, but they contain dust clouds which show up as dark patches. Spiral galaxies come in a wide variety. Some are similar to lenticulars, but have faint spiral arms outside their bulge. The other extreme is a spiral with very long arms but no indication of a central bulge. Irregular spiral arms mark the transition to the irregular galaxies which do not fit into any of the other groups. There are more differentiated classification schemes, which also distinguish barred spirals from standard spirals. Finer subdivisions of galaxies are not easily observable in amateurs' telescopes.

Oblateness: Most star clusters are more or less circular. On the other hand, planetaries, diffuse nebulae, and galaxies can be quite elongated. For these nebulae the tables give their oblateness, which is commonly used only for elliptical galaxies. The scale goes from 0 = circular, to 9 = extremely elongated. A spiral galaxy of oblateness zero is face-on with a good view onto its spiral arms. At oblateness nine we see it edge-on with the best view of dark dust features.

Among the stars there are variable stars. On the other hand, nebulae do not change their light and shape, with two exceptions: Hubble's Variable Nebula (see p. 66) and the expanding light echo of the supernova 1987A near the Tarantula Nebula (see p. 104). It is not known how bright it will develop within the coming years. Time will tell.

Further Reading

Sky Atlas 2000.0 by Wil Tirion. Cambridge University Press and Sky Publishing Corporation, 1981.
This large-format atlas with 43,000 stars to visual magnitude $8^m_.0$ plus 2,500 deep-sky objects is the ideal supplement for the advanced observer.

Sky Catalogue 2000.0 (2 vols.) edited by Alan Hirshfeld and Roger W. Sinnott. Cambridge University Press and Sky Publishing Corporation, 1982 (Vol. 1), 1985 (Vol. 2).
Data and notes on nearly all of the stars and objects of *Sky Atlas 2000.0* are given in this catalog for the advanced observer.

Star Charts and Catalog

NEBULA Designation: number = NGC (New General Catalogue), IC = Index Catalogue, M = Messier.

Const. Constellation abbreviations are listed on pages 128, 129.

Mag. Total visual magnitude and surface brightness (unit area $5'$ across). Low surface brightness (10^m–12^m) needs very dark sky.

Size Apparent diameter of a nebula in arc minutes ($'$).

Shape }
Type } See Table 5 on page 19.

Vis. Visibility under dark sky: ey/Ey unaided eye; op/Op opera glasses; bn/Bn binoculars; tl/Tl amateur telescope (up to 200mm = 8 in. aperture). Capital letter objects are slightly more difficult (see also Table 2, p. 11).

Dist. Distance in light-years (M = million).

R.A. Right ascension for the epoch 2000.0, in hours and minutes.

Dec. Declination for the epoch 2000.0, in degrees.

STAR Designation usually consists of the Flamsteed number and/or the Bayer Greek letter followed by the constellation.

Mag. Visual magnitude V; combined magnitude for double stars.

Spec. Spectral type and luminosity class. Spectral types are O, B, A, F, G, K, M, C from bluish to orange, divided into tenths by the numbers 0 to 9. Luminosity classes are Ia, Ib, II, III, IV, V from supergiants to main sequence stars.

Dist. Distance in light-years.

R.A. Right ascension in the equinox 2000.0, in hours and minutes.

Dec. Declination in the equinox 2000.0, in degrees.

BINARY Designation usually consists of the Flamsteed number and/or the Bayer Greek letter followed by the constellation.

Mag. Visual magnitude V for each component.

Spec. Spectral types are O, B, A, F, G, K, M, C from bluish to orange, divided into tenths by the numbers 0 to 9. Beautiful color contrast is marked by "!".

PA Position angle of companion, counterclockwise from north, for the period 1990–2010.

Sep. Separation from primary in arc seconds (C: from companion).

Vis. Visibility: ey/Ey unaided eye; op/Op opera glasses; bn/Bn binoculars; tl/Tl telescope (up to 200mm aperture). Capital-letter objects are slightly more difficult (see Table 2, p. 11).

VARIABLE STAR Types are listed in Table 4, p. 17.

Max./Min. Time of maximum/minimum; phase = phase in light curve, goes from zero to one between two maxima/minima.

Mean Mean magnitude or magnitude range.

Arrangement of Charts

Season	Northern Sky	Equator, Ecliptic	Southern Sky
Late fall	N0 – N4	E0 – E2	S0
Winter	N4 – N8	E2 – E10	S3 – S6
Spring	N8 – N14	E9 – E16	S6 – S18
Summer	N14 – N22	E15 – E22	S18 – S24
Early fall	N22 – N24	E22 – E24	S24

Charts E0–E24 of the equator and ecliptic alternate between more southerly (E0, E2, E4, ...) and more northerly regions (E1, E3, ...).

The seasons refer to the earth's northern hemisphere. They need to be reversed for observers in the southern hemisphere.

STAR		Mag.	Spec.	Name, Comments	Dist.	R.A.	Dec.
48	Cas	4.5	d A4 V	. . . .	100ly	$2^h 02.0$	$+70.91$
50	Cas	4.0	A1 V	. . . .	120	2 03.4	$+72.42$
1	α UMi	2.0	F8 Ib	**Polaris**, North Star .	800	2 31.8	$+89.26$
78	Cam	4.8	d A1 III	sometimes called Σ1694	400	12 49.2	$+83.41$
5	UMi	4.3	K4 III	. . . .	250	14 27.5	$+75.70$
7	β UMi	2.1	K4 III	Kochab	100	14 50.7	$+74.16$
13	γ UMi	3.1	A3 II	Pherkad	200	15 20.7	$+71.83$
16	ζ UMi	4.3	A3 V	. . . .	120	15 44.1	$+77.79$
21	η UMi	5.0	F4 V	. . . .	80	16 17.5	$+75.76$
22	ε UMi	4.2	G5 III	. . . .	200	16 46.0	$+82.04$
23	δ UMi	4.4	A1 V	. . . .	150	17 32.2	$+86.59$
41	Dra	5.1	d F7 V	companion is 40 Dra	100	18 00.1	$+80.00$
75	Dra	5.2	d G9 III	. . . .	400	20 27.9	$+81.43$

BINARY		Mag.	Spec.		PA	Sep.	Vis.	Coordinates of Polaris		
48	Cas	$4.7\ 6.4$	A3 F2	'90	$234°$	$0.9''$	Tl	1900.0	$1^h 22.6$	$+88.77$
				2000	263	0.9	Tl	1950.0	1 48.8	$+89.03$
				2010	299	0.7	-	1990.0	2 21.3	$+89.22$
78	Cam	5.3 5.8	A2 A0		326	21.6	Bn	2000.0	2 31.8	$+89.26$
41	Dra	5.7 6.0	F7 F7		231	18.8	tl	2010.0	2 43.6	$+89.31$
75	Dra	5.5 6.7	G9 G9		282	197	Op	2050.0	3 47.5	$+89.46$

Stellar diameters and scale in star charts

−1ᵐ 0ᵐ 1ᵐ 2ᵐ 3ᵐ 4ᵐ 5ᵐ 6ᵐ   0° 5° 10° 15° 20°

2ᵐ 3ᵐ 4ᵐ 5ᵐ 6ᵐ 7ᵐ 8ᵐ 9ᵐ   0° 1° 2° 3° 4° 5°

in round enlarged sections

Stellar magnitudes in tenths of a magnitude (20 = 2ᵐ0, etc.)

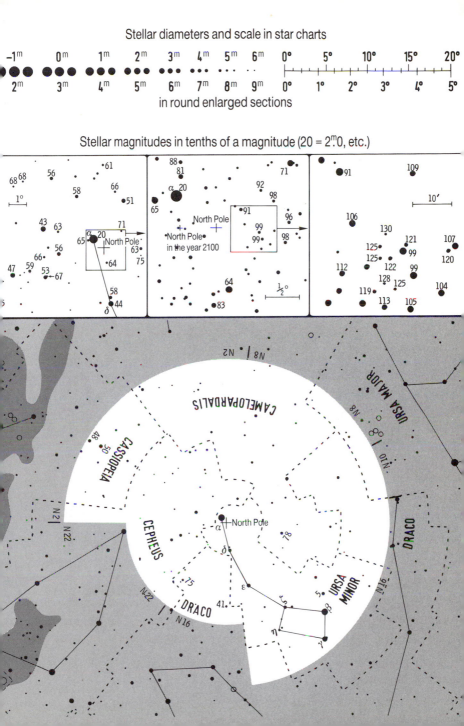

NEBULA	Const.	Mag.		Size	Shape		Type	Vis.	Dist.	R.A.	Dec.
205	M110	And	9^m	$10^m_{(5')}$	10'	E	5	Galx	bn	2.5 Mly	0^h40^m	+41°.7
221	M32	And	8½	8	4	E	2	Galx	Op	2.5 M	0 43	+40.9
224	M31	And	4	10	150	Sb	7	Galx	ey	2.5 M	0 43	+41.3
598	M33	Tri	6	11	50	Sc	4	Galx	op	3 M	1 34	+30.7
650	M76	Per	11	9	2.5	A	5	Plan	tl	5000	1 42	+51.6
752		And	5½	10	50	m		Open	Ey	2000	1 58	+37.7
891		And	10½	10	12	Sb	9	Galx	Bn	30 M	2 23	+42.3

205	M110	companion galaxy of the Andromeda Galaxy, slightly asymmetric
221	M32	companion of the Andromeda Galaxy, stellar in binoculars
224	M31	**Andromeda Galaxy**, nearest large galaxy, physically comparable with our Milky Way, bright core, dust lanes west of the core, outer spiral arms and great size visible under dark sky
598	M33	**Triangulum Galaxy**, dark sky and low magnification essential, spiral arms with emission nebulae and stellar associations visible in large telescopes
650	M76	**Little Dumbbell**, faintest Messier object (NGC 650, 651)
752		difficult with unaided eye, nicely resolved in binoculars
891		faint edge-on galaxy, shape very distinct in a large telescope

STAR			Mag.	Spec.	Name, Comments	Dist.	R.A.	Dec.
21	α	And	2.0	B 9 IV	**Alpheratz, Sirrah** . .	90 ly	$0^h08^m.4$	+29°.09
31	δ	And	3.3	K3 III	. . . .	150	0 39.3	+30.86
35	ν	And	4.5	B5 V	. . . .	400	0 49.8	+41.08
37	μ	And	3.9	A5 V	. . . .	80	0 56.8	+38.50
43	β	And	2.1	M0 III	**Mirach**	90	1 09.7	+35.62
50	υ	And	4.1	F8 V	. . . .	45	1 36.8	+41.41
51		And	3.6	K3 III	. . . .	200	1 38.0	+48.63
	φ	Per	4.1	B2 V	. . . .	1000	1 43.7	+50.69
2	α	Tri	3.4	F6 IV	Elmuthalleth . . .	60	1 53.1	+29.58
56		And	5.0	d K2 III	. . . .	250	1 56.0	+37.26
57	γ	And	2.2	d K1 III	**Alamak**	300	2 03.9	+42.33
4	β	Tri	3.0	A5 III	. . . .	120	2 09.5	+34.99
59		And	5.5	d A0 V	. . . .	300	2 10.9	+39.04
6	ι	Tri	4.9	d G3 III	not always designated	300	2 12.4	+30.30
9	γ	Tri	4.0	A0 V	. . . . ⌊ι Tri⌋	150	2 17.3	+33.85
15		Tri	5.1	d K6 III	. . . .	400	2 35.8	+34.70
R		Tri	5.4–12.6	M4 III	. . . .	600	2 37.0	+34.26

BINARY			Mag.		Spec.		PA	Sep.	Vis.
56		And	5.7	5.9	K0	K4	299°	200″	op
57	γ	And	2.2	5.0	K3!	B9	63	9.6	tl
59		And	6.0	6.5	B9	A1	35	16.6	tl
6	ι	Tri	5.2	6.8	G5	F5	69	3.9	tl
15		Tri	5.4	6.8	M4!	A5	17	143	Op

VARIABLE STAR	
R Tri	Mira type
Period	266.7 d
Max.	2448148
Min.	phase 0.56
Mean	$6^m.2–11^m.7$

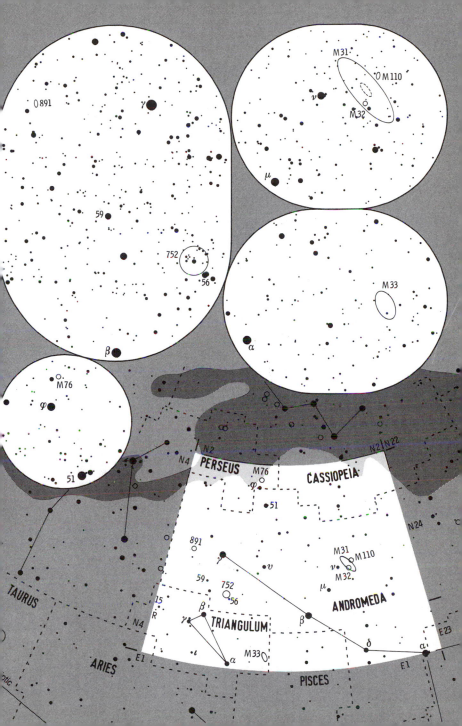

891

γ

59

752

56

β

M31

M110

ν

M32

μ

M33

α

M76

φ

51

N2

N4 PERSEUS M76 CASSIOPEIA
φ
51

N2 N22

N24

891
γ ν
59 752
56
15
R
β TRIANGULUM
γ
TAURUS

M31 M110
ν
M32
μ
ANDROMEDA
β
δ
α

N4
E1
ι α M33

ARIES

E1

PISCES

E23

E1

NEBULA	Const.	Mag.		Size	Shape	Type	Vis.	Dist.	R.A.	Dec.
281	Cas	8^m	11$^m_{(5')}$	25$'$	Em2	Diff	bn	6000 ly	0^{h}53^m	+56°6
457	Cas	7	9	12	r	Open	op	6000	1 19	+58.3
559	Cas	8	8	6	m	Open	Op	6000	1 29	+63.3
581	M103 Cas	7½	8	6	p	Open	op	6000	1 33	+60.7
654	Cas	8	8	5	m	Open	Op	8000	1 44	+61.9
663	Cas	7	9	12	m	Open	op	6000	1 46	+61.3
869	Per	4½	8	25	r	Open	ey	8000	2 19	+57.1
884	Per	4½	8	25	r	Open	ey	8000	2 22	+57.1

281		faint in binoculars, interesting in a telescope with nebular filter
457		the brightest stars are well resolved in binoculars
559		looks like a faint nebula in binoculars, resolved in a telescope
581	M103	partially resolved in binoculars, not much better in a telescope
654		contains many faint stars, therefore mostly nebulous appearance
663		excellent even in binoculars, many individual stars,
		irregular shape, contains two regions with many faint stars
869		h Persei ⎫ **Double Cluster, h and χ Persei,**
884		χ Persei ⎭ relatively easily visible with unaided eye,
		splendid view in binoculars, still better in a telescope at low
		magnification, each cluster contains approximately 300 stars

STAR			Mag.	Spec.	Name, Comments		Dist.	R.A.	Dec.
11	β	Cas	2^{m}3	F 2 IV	Chaph	. . . . . .	45 ly	0^{h}09^{m}2	+59°15
14	λ	Cas	4.7	d B8 V	. . . .		300	0 31.8	+54.52
17	ζ	Cas	3.7	B 2 IV	. . . .		600	0 37.0	+53.90
18	α	Cas	2.2	K0 III	Schedir	. . . . .	120	0 40.5	+56.54
24	η	Cas	3.4	d G0 V	. . . .		19	0 49.1	+57.82
27	γ	Cas	1.6–3.0	B0 IV	. . . .		800	0 56.7	+60.72
34	φ	Cas	4.8	d A8 Ia	. . . .		10000	1 20.1	+58.23
37	δ	Cas	2.7	A5 IV	Ruchbah	. . . . .	80	1 25.8	+60.24
45	ε	Cas	3.4	B3 III	. . . .		500	1 54.4	+63.67
	ι	Cas	4.5	d A5 V	. . . .		150	2 29.1	+67.40
SU		Cas	5.7–6.2	F 6 Ib	. . . .		4000	2 52.0	+68.89
9	α	Cam	4.3	O9 Ia	. . . .		3000	4 54.1	+66.34
10	β	Cam	4.0	d F9 Ib	. . . .		1500	5 03.4	+60.44
11		Cam	4.8	d A2 V	companion is 12 Cam		600	5 06.2	+58.98

BINARY			Mag.	Spec.	PA	Sep.	Vis.
14	λ	Cas	5^{m}3 5^{m}6	B8 B9	191°	0″6	-
24	η	Cas	3.5 7.5	G0!M0 '90	312	12.5	tl
				2010	322	13.2	tl
34	φ	Cas	5.0 7.0	F0 B5	231	134	Op
	ι	Cas	4.6 6.9	A4 F 5	230	2.5	tl
10	β	Cam	4.0 7.4	G0 A5	208	81	bn
11		Cam	5.1 6.3	B3!K0	8	180	op

VARIABLE STAR		
27 γ Cas		irregular
	Period	> 1 d
	Mean	≈ 2^{m}5
SU Cas		Cepheid
	Period	1.94932 d
	Max.	2447893.39
	Min.	phase 0.60

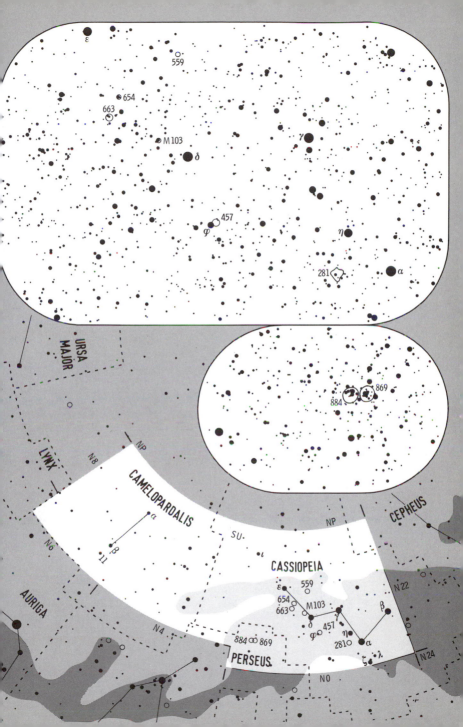

NEBULA	Const.	Mag.	Size	Shape	Type	Vis.	Dist.	R.A.	Dec.
1023	Per	10^m $9^m_{(5')}$	$5'$	L 7	Galx	Bn	30 Mly	$2^h40\frac{1}{2}^m$	$+39°.1$
1039 M34	Per	6 9	25	m	Open	Ey	1500	2 42	+42.8
1245	Per	8½ 11	15	r	Open	bn	8000	3 15	+47.3
1491	Per	10 9	3	Em0	Diff	Bn	2500	4 03	+51.3
1528	Per	6½ 10	25	m	Open	op	2500	4 15	+51.2

1023   faint elliptical nebula without features in amateur telescopes

1039 M34   very nice cluster for binoculars, interesting in a telescope at low
magnification only, deficiency of faint stars,
some stars seem to be aligned along arms

1245   faint nebula in binoculars, individual stars become visible in
large telescopes, nebulous background from many faint stars

1491   at high power with nebular filter well separated from 11^m star

1528   interesting cluster in every telescope, some individual stars are
visible in binoculars, irregular distribution of faint stars

STAR		Mag.	Spec.	Name, Comments	Dist.	R.A.	Dec.
16	Per	$4^m.2$	F 2 III	. . . .	150 ly	$2^h50^m.6$	$+38°.32$
15	η Per	3.8	K7 Ib	. . . .	800	2 50.7	+55.90
18	τ Per	4.0	G4 III	. . . .	200	2 54.3	+52.76
23	γ Per	2.9	G8 III	. . . .	150	3 04.8	+53.51
25	ϱ Per	3.3–4.0	M4 III	. . . .	200	3 05.2	+38.84
26	β Per	2.1–3.4	B8 V	**Algol**	90	3 08.2	+40.96
	ι Per	4.1	G0 V	. . . .	35	3 09.1	+49.61
27	κ Per	3.8	K0 III	. . . .	150	3 09.5	+44.86
33	α Per	1.8	F 5 Ib	**Mirphak**	600	3 24.3	+49.86
39	δ Per	3.0	B5 III	. . . .	300	3 42.9	+47.79
38	o Per	3.8	B1 III	Atik	1000	3 44.3	+32.29
41	ν Per	3.8	F5 II	. . . .	400	3 45.2	+42.58
44	ζ Per	2.9	B1 Ib	. . . .	1200	3 54.1	+31.88
45	ε Per	2.9	d B0 V	. . . .	600	3 57.9	+40.01
46	ξ Per	4.0	O7 V	Menkib	1500	3 59.0	+35.79
48	υ Per	4.0	B3 V	. . . .	400	4 08.7	+47.71
51	μ Per	4.1	G0 Ib	. . . .	1500	4 14.9	+48.41
1	Cam	5.4	d B0 III	. . . .	3000	4 32.0	+53.91
57	Per	5.6	d F0 V	. . . .	200	4 33.4	+43.05
2	Cam	5.4	d F1 V	. . . .	120	4 40.0	+53.47

BINARY		Mag.	Spec.		PA	Sep.	Vis.
45	ε Per	$2^m.9$ $7^m.4$	B0	A0	10°	$8''.8$	tl
1	Cam	5.8 6.9	B0	B0	308	10.3	tl
57	Per	6.1 6.8	F0	F0	197	122	Op
2	Cam	5.6 7.3	F0	F8 '90	213	0.7	-
				2000	194	0.7	-
				2010	174	0.7	-

VARIABLE STAR

25 ϱ Per   semiregular
    Period   ≈ 50 d

26 β Per   **Algol**
    Period   2.86731 d
    Min.   2447895.22
    Max. ph.0.07–0.93

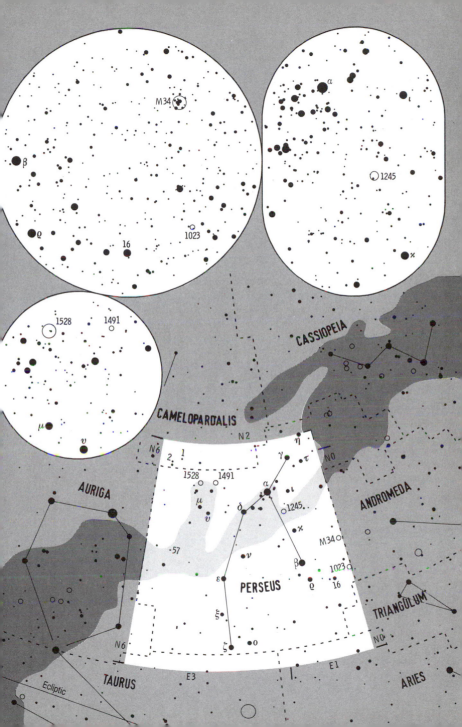

M34

1245

1528   1491

1023

β

ϱ

16

CASSIOPEIA

CAMELOPARDALIS

N 2

N 6   2   1

1528   1491

μ

ν

AURIGA

57

δ

η

γ   τ

α   ι

1245

χ

ν

β

ϱ   16

M34

1023

ANDROMEDA

PERSEUS

ε

ξ

ζ   o

N 6

μ

ν

TRIANGULUM

TAURUS

Ecliptic

E 3

N 0

N 0

E 1

ARIES

NEBULA		Const.	Mag.		Size	Shape	Type	Vis.	Dist.	R.A.	Dec.
1912	M38	Aur	7^m	$10^m_{(5')}$	$20'$	m	Open	op	4000 ly	5^h29^m	$+35°.8$
1931		Aur	10	9	3	Em0	Diff	Bn	4000	5 31½	+34.2
1960	M36	Aur	6½	8	12	m	Open	Ey	4000	5 36	+34.1
2099	M37	Aur	6	9	20	r	Open	Ey	4000	5 52	+32.5
2281		Aur	6½	9	15	p	Open	op	2500	6 49	+41.1

1912	M38	partially resolved in binoculars, interesting grouping of faint stars
1931		small faint diffuse nebula, imbedded stars visible at high power
1960	M36	resolved even in binoculars, deficiency of faint stars, stellar groupings along arms
2099	M37	binoculars show a large bright glow, which turns into an amazing number of stars in large telescopes
2281		cluster consisting of bright, irregularly scattered stars

STAR			Mag.	Spec.	Name, Comments	Dist.	R.A.	Dec.
3	ι	Aur	$2^m.7$	K3 II	. . . .	250 ly	$4^h57^m.0$	$+33°.17$
4	ω	Aur	4.9	d A0 V	. . . .	250	4 59.3	+37.89
7	ε	Aur	2.9–3.8	F0 Ia	. . . .	4000	5 02.0	+43.82
8	ζ	Aur	3.7–4.0	K4 II	. . . .	500	5 02.5	+41.08
10	η	Aur	3.2	B3 V	. . . .	200	5 06.5	+41.23
14		Aur	5.0	d A9 IV	. . . .	200	5 15.4	+32.69
13	α	Aur	0.1	G5 III	Capella	40	5 16.7	+46.00
26		Aur	5.3	d F0 III	. . . .	500	5 38.6	+30.49
32	ν	Aur	4.0	K0 III	. . . .	150	5 51.5	+39.15
33	δ	Aur	3.7	K0 III	. . . .	150	5 59.5	+54.28
34	β	Aur	1.9	A2 IV	Menkalinan	70	5 59.5	+44.95
37	ϑ	Aur	2.6	A0 III	. . . .	150	5 59.7	+37.21
41		Aur	5.8	d A4 V	. . . .	250	6 11.6	+48.71
5		Lyn	5.1	d K4 III	. . . .	400	6 26.8	+58.42
48		Aur	5.0–5.8	F9 Ib	RT Aurigae	2500	6 28.6	+30.49
12		Lyn	4.8	d A2 IV	. . . .	300	6 46.2	+59.44
15		Lyn	4.4	d G5 III	. . . .	150	6 57.3	+58.42
19		Lyn	5.1	d B8 V	. . . .	400	7 22.9	+55.28

BINARY			Mag.		Spec.		PA	Sep.	Vis.
4	ω	Aur	$4^m.9$	$7^m.8$	A0	F5	$2°$	$5''.0$	tl
14		Aur	5.1	7.5	A9	F	226	14.6	tl
26		Aur	5.4	8.0	F0	F0	267	12.4	tl
41		Aur	6.2	7.0	A3	A7	357	7.6	tl
5		Lyn	5.2	7.8	K4	G8	272	96	bn
12		Lyn	5.4	6.0	A2	A2 '90	75	1.7	tl
						2010	65	1.7	tl
				7.3		A8	308	8.7	tl
15		Lyn	4.7	5.8	G5	G	45	1.0	Tl
19		Lyn	5.5	6.5	B8	B9	315	14.8	tl

VARIABLE STAR

7 ε Aur	Algol type
Max.	1985–2009
8 ζ Aur	Algol type
Period	972.16 d
Min.	2448108.2
Max. ph.0.02–0.98	
48 RT Aur	Cepheid
Period	3.7281 d
Max.	2447893.7
Min.	phase 0.75

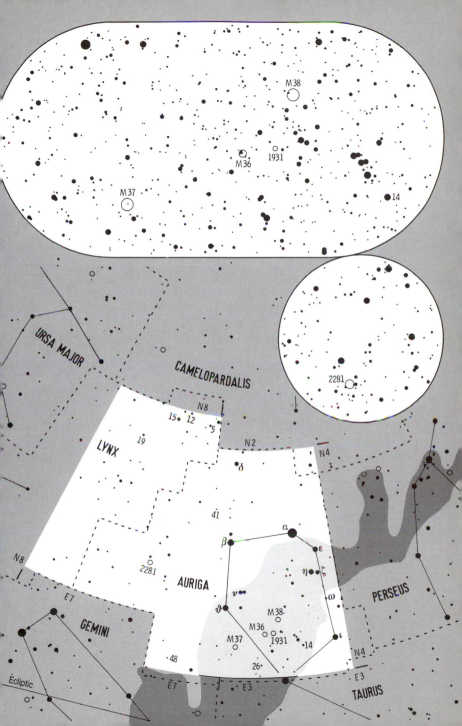

NEBULA	Const.	Mag.		Size	Shape	Type	Vis.	Dist.	R.A.	Dec.
2403	Cam	$8\frac{1}{2}^m$	$10^m_{(5')}$	12$'$	Sc 4	Galx	bn	10 Mly	7^h37^m	$+65\overset{\circ}{.}6$
2683	Lyn	10	9	8	Sb 8	Galx	Bn	10 M	8 53	+33.4
2841	UMa	$9\frac{1}{2}$	10	8	Sb 6	Galx	Bn	30 M	9 22	+51.0
2976	UMa	$10\frac{1}{2}$	9	4	Sc 6	Galx	Bn	10 M	9 47	+67.9
3031 M81	UMa	7	9	20	Sb 5	Galx	op	10 M	9 56	+69.1
3034 M82	UMa	$8\frac{1}{2}$	9	10	Ir 6	Galx	Op	10 M	9 56	+69.7
3077	UMa	$10\frac{1}{2}$	9	3	Ir 2	Galx	Bn	10 M	10 03	+68.7

2403		seen well in binoculars, spiral arms dim in large telescopes
2683		faint edge-on galaxy, dust features in a large telescope only
2841		small bright core within an elongated nebula
2976		companion galaxy of M81, elliptical in amateur telescopes
3031	M81	central galaxy in a group of galaxies, easily visible in binoculars, bright central region with stellar core, faint detail
3034	M82	brightest companion of M81, only 37$'$ north, active galaxy, nearly edge-on, wonderful features in a large telescope
3077		companion galaxy of M81, featureless nebula with bright core

STAR		Mag.	Spec.	Name, Comments	Dist.	R.A.	Dec.
31	Lyn	$4\overset{m}{.}3$	K5 III	. . . .	200ly	$8^h22\overset{m}{.}8$	$+43\overset{\circ}{.}19$
1	o UMa	3.3–3.8	G5 III	. . . .	200	8 30.3	+60.72
9	ι UMa	3.1	A7 V	Talitha	50	8 59.2	+48.04
10	UMa	4.0	F5 V	in Lynx	50	9 00.6	+41.78
12	κ UMa	3.6	A0 V	. . . .	120	9 03.6	+47.16
38	Lyn	3.8	d A4 V	. . . .	90	9 18.8	+36.80
40	α Lyn	3.1	K9 III	. . . .	150	9 21.1	+34.39
41	Lyn	5.3	d G7 IV	in Ursa Major . . .	150	9 28.7	+45.60
23	UMa	3.7	F0 IV	. . . .	80	9 31.5	+63.06
25	ϑ UMa	3.2	F6 IV	. . . .	50	9 32.9	+51.68
24	UMa	4.6	G3 IV	. . . .	80	9 34.5	+69.83
29	υ UMa	3.8	F2 IV	. . . .	80	9 51.0	+59.04
31	β LMi	4.2	G9 III	. . . .	200	10 27.9	+36.71
46	LMi	3.8	K0 III	also designated o LMi	80	10 53.3	+34.21

Constellation Boundaries (dashed in star charts): At the time Flamsteed numbered the stars 300 years ago, there were no fixed boundaries between constellations. Not until 1930 were they defined by the International Astronomical Union. A few stars were too far away from their constellation or shared two constellations. Thus in 1930 they were assigned to another constellation. For this reason 10 Ursae Majoris and 41 Lyncis are not located within the constellation of their Flamsteed designation.

BINARY		Mag.	Spec.	PA	Sep.	Vis.
38	Lyn	$3\overset{m}{.}9$ $6\overset{m}{.}4$	A2 G0	226$°$	2$\overset{''}{.}$7	tl
41	Lyn	5.4 7.9	G8 F9	162	70	bn

VARIABLE STAR

1	o UMa	type ?
	Period	358 d ?

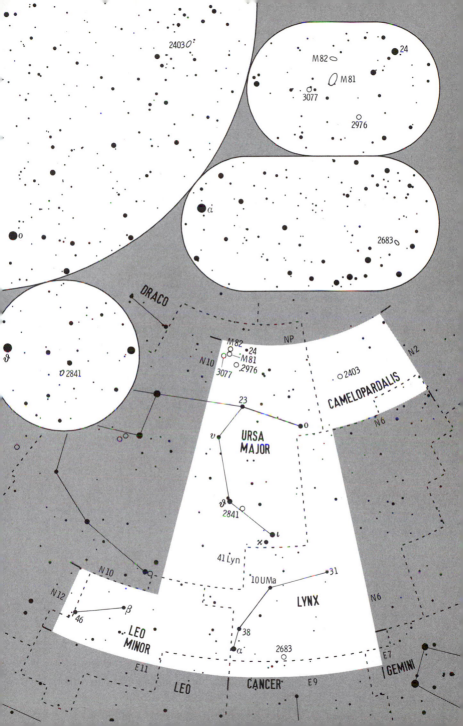

NEBULA		Const.	Mag.		Size	Shape Type		Vis.	Dist.	R.A.	Dec.
3184		UMa	10^m	$10^m_{(5')}$	$6'$	Sc 2	Galx	Bn	25 Mly	10^h18^m	$+41°.4$
3556	M108	UMa	10	9	8	Sc 8	Galx	Bn	30 M	11 11	+55.7
3587	M97	UMa	11	10	3	D 0	Plan	tl	3000	11 15	+55.0
3992	M109	UMa	10	10	6	Sb 4	Galx	Bn	40 M	11 58	+53.4
	M40	UMa	8½	(4)	0.8	Double Star		bn	500	12 22½	+58.1
5457	M101	UMa	8	11	20	Sc 1	Galx	bn	15 M	14 03	+54.4

3184		faint, spiral structure not observable in amateur telescopes
3556	M108	distinct edge-on galaxy, a hint of features in large telescopes
3587	M97	**Owl Nebula**, both dark eyes not quite visible in amateur telescopes
3992	M109	faint nebula with nonstellar central condensation
	M40	double star, two 9^m stars at $50''$ separation, which exactly matches Messier's description, it is certainly the correct identification
5457	M101	**Pinwheel Galaxy**, often just the bright central core is visible, only with darkest sky and lowest power does the enormous size becomes apparent, unfortunately the beautiful spiral arms are not well visible in amateur telescopes

STAR			Mag.	Spec.	Name, Comments	Dist.	R.A.	Dec.
33	λ	UMa	$3^m.5$	A2 IV	Tania Borealis . . .	120ly	$10^h17^m.1$	+42°.91
34	μ	UMa	3.1	M0 III	Tania Australis . .	150	10 22.3	+41.50
VY		UMa	5.9–6.5	C5 II	. . . .	2500	10 45.1	+67.41
48	β	UMa	2.4	A1 V	**Merak**	60	11 01.8	+56.38
50	α	UMa	1.8	K0 III	**Dubhe**	80	11 03.7	+61.75
52	ψ	UMa	3.0	K1 III	. . . .	120	11 09.7	+44.50
63	χ	UMa	3.7	K1 III	. . . .	120	11 46.1	+47.78
64	γ	UMa	2.4	A0 V	**Phegda, Phad** . .	70	11 53.8	+53.69
69	δ	UMa	3.3	A3 V	**Megrez**	60	12 15.4	+57.03
77	ε	UMa	1.8	A0 IV	**Alioth**	80	12 54.0	+55.96
78		UMa	4.9	d F3 V	. . . .	90	13 00.7	+56.37
79	ζ	UMa	2.1	d A2 V	**Mizar** } Sep. $11''.8$	70	13 23.9	+54.93
80		UMa	4.0	A5 V	**Alcor** }	70	13 25.2	+54.99
85	η	UMa	1.9	B3 V	**Alkaid, Benetnasch** .	120	13 47.5	+49.31

Mizar, Alcor: This binary is often called the horse and rider. Its 11.8 arc-minutes separation is much greater than the limit of resolution of the eye with normal vision (approximately $5'$). Therefore, Alcor should be well visible when the sky is dark enough. Other stars testing the resolution of the unaided eye are ϑ Tau (chart E3), α Cap = Algiedi (E22), μ Sco (S21), and δ Gru (S24).

BINARY		Mag.	Spec.	PA	Sep.	Vis.		VARIABLE STAR
78	UMa	$5^m.1$ $7^m.4$	F2 G6 '90	$57°$	$1''.5$	Tl		VY UMa irregular
			2000	69	1.5	Tl		one of the
			2010	82	1.4	Tl		reddest stars
79	ζ UMa	2.3 4.0	A2 A2	153	14.4	tl		in the sky

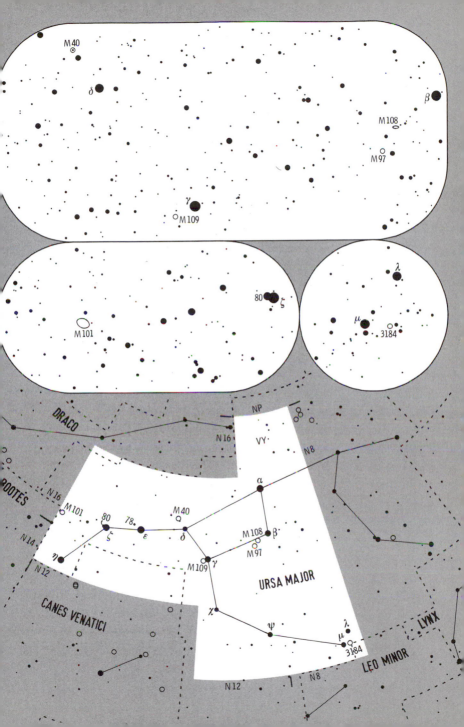

NEBULA		Const.	Mag.		Size	Shape	Type	Vis.	Dist.	R.A.	Dec.
4244		CVn	$10\frac{1}{2}^m$	$11\frac{m}{(5')}$	15'	Sc 9	Galx	tl	20 M ly	12^h17^m	$+37°8$
4258	M106	CVn	$8\frac{1}{2}$	10	12	Sb 6	Galx	bn	20 M	12 19	+47.3
4449		CVn	$9\frac{1}{2}$	9	4	Ir 3	Galx	Bn	20 M	12 28	+44.1
4490		CVn	10	9	5	Sd 6	Galx	Bn	20 M	$12\ 30\frac{1}{2}$	+41.6
4736	M94	CVn	$8\frac{1}{2}$	9	6	Sb 3	Galx	Op	20 M	12 51	+41.1
5055	M63	CVn	9	10	10	Sb 5	Galx	bn	20 M	13 16	+42.0
5194	M51	CVn	$8\frac{1}{2}$	10	10	Sb 2	Galx	bn	20 M	13 30	+47.2
5195		CVn	10	9	3	Ir 2	Galx	Bn	20 M	13 30	+47.3

4244		very faint galaxy, but intriguing edge-on shape
4258	M106	elliptical glow in a small telescope, in large telescopes faint dust features become visible, traces of spiral arms
4449		approximately rectangular, but asymmetric shape, bright central region, dust clouds visible in large telescopes
4490		elongated central region within a large faint background glow
4736	M94	bright core, hints of spiral arms in large telescopes
5055	M63	nonstellar core, spiral arms too faint for amateur telescopes
5194	M51	**Whirlpool Galaxy**, wonderful spiral arms become visible in large telescopes, one arm is winding towards NGC 5195, this might be the most beautiful spiral in the sky
5195		probably companion of M51, already visible in small telescopes as the fainter one of the two nebulae

STAR			Mag.	Spec.	Name, Comments	Dist.	R.A.	Dec.
53	ξ	UMa	3.8	d G0 V	Alula Australis . . .	25 ly	$11^h18.2$	$+31°53$
54	ν	UMa	3.5	K3 III	Alula Borealis . . .	150	11 18.5	+33.09
8	β	CVn	4.3	G0 V	. . . .	30	12 33.7	+41.36
Y		CVn	5.5–6.0	C6 Ib	La Superba	4000	12 45.1	+45.44
12	α	CVn	2.8	d A1 IV	Cor Caroli	120	12 56.0	+38.32
17		CVn	5.0	d A9 III	far companion is 15 CVn	400	13 10.1	+38.50
25		CVn	4.8	d A7 III	. . . .	200	13 37.5	+36.29

BINARY			Mag.		Spec.		PA	Sep.	Vis.
53	ξ	UMa	4.3	4.8	G0	G0 '90	60°	1.3	Tl
						1992	25	0.9	Tl
						1994	335	0.9	Tl
		minimum separation				1996	304	1.3	Tl
		0.8 in November 1992,				1998	286	1.6	tl
		rotation 2° per month				2000	273	1.8	tl
						2005	243	1.7	tl
						2010	208	1.6	tl
12	α	CVn	2.9	5.6	A0	F 0	229	19.4	tl
17		CVn	5.9	6.2	A9	B9	296	79	bn
				6.3		B 7	297	278	op
25		CVn	5.0	6.9	A7	F 0	99	1.8	Tl

VARIABLE STAR

Y CVn semiregular
Period ≈ 157 d
one of the
reddest stars,
spectral type C
= carbon star,
especially red at
minimum bright-
ness, color
becomes very
distinct only in
large telescopes

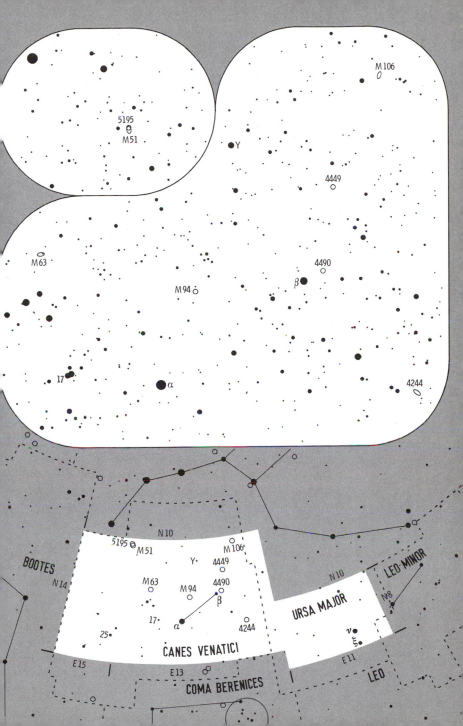

NEBULA		Const.	Mag.	Size	Shape	Type	Vis.	Dist.	R.A.	Dec.
6205	M13	Her	6^m	8$^m_{(5')}$ 15$'$	V	Glob	Ey	25000ly	16^{h}42^m	+36°5
6341	M92	Her	6½	8	8	IV	Glob	op	30000	17 17	+43.1

6205 M13 **Hercules Cluster**, bright nebula in binoculars, outer portion well resolved in a telescope at high power, center more difficult

6341 M92 similar to M13, outer stars resolved in large telescopes

STAR			Mag.	Spec.	Name, Comments	Dist.	R.A.	Dec.
17	κ	Boo	4^{m}4	d A 7 IV	. . . .	150ly	14^{h}13^{m}5	+51°79
21	ι	Boo	4.7	d A 8 V	. . . .	100	14 16.2	+51.37
23	ϑ	Boo	4.1	F 7 V	. . . .	45	14 25.2	+51.85
27	γ	Boo	3.0	A 7 III	Ceginus	100	14 32.1	+38.31
39		Boo	5.7	d F 6 V	. . . .	150	14 49.7	+48.72
42	β	Boo	3.5	G 8 III	Nekkar	150	15 01.9	+40.39
44		Boo	4.8–4.9	d F 9 V	i Bootis	40	15 03.8	+47.65
49	δ	Boo	3.5	G 8 III	. . . .	150	15 15.5	+33.31
51	μ	Boo	4.2	d F 2 IV	Alkalurops	100	15 24.5	+37.37
7	ζ	CrB	4.7	d B 7 V	. . . .	400	15 39.4	+36.64
11	φ	Her	4.3	B 9 V	. . . .	200	16 08.8	+44.93
17	σ	CrB	5.2	d G 0 V	. . . .	70	16 14.7	+33.86
22	τ	Her	3.9	B 5 IV	. . . .	400	16 19.7	+46.31
30		Her	4.3–6.3	M 6 III	g Herculis	400	16 28.6	+41.88
35	σ	Her	4.2	B 9 V	. . . .	200	16 34.1	+42.44
40	ζ	Her	2.8	G 0 IV	. . . .	32	16 41.3	+31.60
44	η	Her	3.5	G 8 III	. . . .	80	16 42.9	+38.92
58	ε	Her	3.9	A 0 V	. . . .	100	17 00.3	+30.93
67	π	Her	3.2	K 3 II	. . . .	400	17 15.0	+36.81
68		Her	4.7–5.4	B 3 III	u Herculis	1200	17 17.3	+33.10
75	ϱ	Her	4.1	d A 0 III	. . . .	300	17 23.7	+37.15
85	ι	Her	3.8	B 3 IV	. . . .	500	17 39.5	+46.01
91	ϑ	Her	3.9	K 1 II	. . . .	400	17 56.3	+37.25

BINARY			Mag.	Spec.	PA	Sep.	Vis.
17	κ	Boo	4^{m}5 6^{m}7	A 7 F 1	236°	13$''$6	tl
21	ι	Boo	4.8 7.7	A 8 A 2	33	38.5	Bn
39		Boo	6.2 6.8	F 6 F 5	45	2.8	tl
44		Boo	5.1 7	F 8 G 2 '90	47	1.7	Tl
				2000	53	2.2	tl
				2010	57	2.3	tl
51	μ	Boo	4.3 7.0	F 1 G 2	171	108	bn
			7.6	G 5	8 C	2.3	tl
7	ζ	CrB	5.0 6.0	B 7 B 8	306	6.3	tl
17	σ	CrB	5.6 6.6	G 0 G 1 '90	235	6.9	tl
				2010	238	7.3	tl
75	ϱ	Her	4.5 5.5	A 0 A 0	319	4.2	tl

VARIABLE STAR

44 i Boo   β Lyr type
  Perd. 0.2678160 d
  Min. 2447892.59
  Magnitudes:
  primary   5^{m}1
  companion 6^{m}5–7^{m}1

30 g Her   semiregular
  Period   70–90 d

68 u Her   β Lyr type
  Period 2.051027 d
  Min. 2447892.50
  Max. ph.≈0.2–0.8

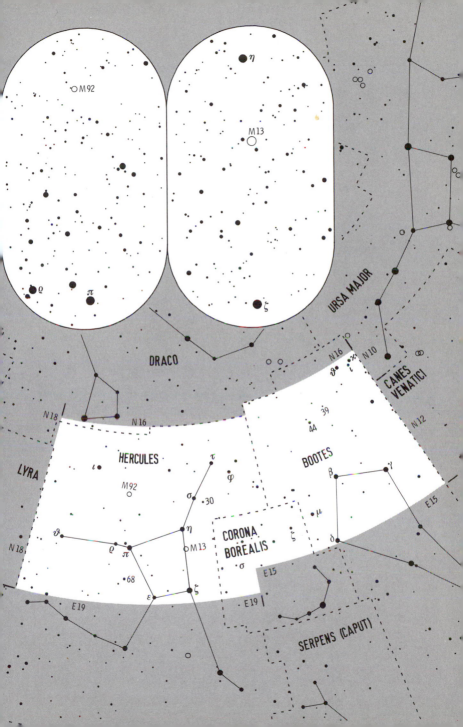

NEBULA		Const.	Mag.		Size	Shape	Type	Vis.	Dist.	R.A.	Dec.
5866	M102	Dra	$10\frac{1}{2}^m$	$9\frac{m}{(5')}$	3'	L 6	Galx	Bn	30 Mly	$15^h06\frac{1}{2}^m$	+55°.8
5907		Dra	$10\frac{1}{2}$	10	10	Sc 9	Galx	tl	30 M	15 16	+56.3
6503		Dra	$10\frac{1}{2}$	9	5	Sc 8	Galx	tl	15 M	17 49	+70.1
6543		Dra	9	4	0.5	D 3	Plan	Op	3000	17 59	+66.6

5866	M102	appears as an elliptic nebula (see also comment at bottom right)
5907		difficult because of low magnitude, but distinct edge-on shape
6503		nearly edge-on galaxy, distinctly elongated, quite far north
6543		relatively easily visible planetary, stellar in binoculars, bright
		greenish ellipse in large telescopes at high magnification

STAR			Mag.	Spec.	Name, Comments	Dist.	R.A.	Dec.
1	λ	Dra	$3.^m8$	M0 III	Giauzar	200ly	$11^h31.^m4$	+69.33
5	κ	Dra	3.9	B6 III	. . . .	400	12 33.5	+69.79
11	α	Dra	3.7	A0 III	Thuban	200	14 04.4	+64.38
12	ι	Dra	3.3	K2 III	Edasich	150	15 24.9	+58.97
13	ϑ	Dra	4.0	F8 IV	. . . .	60	16 01.9	+58.57
14	η	Dra	2.7	G8 III	. . . .	80	16 24.0	+61.51
17		Dra	4.5	dB9 V	far companion is 16 Dra	300	16 36.2	+52.91
21	μ	Dra	4.9	dF7 V	. . . .	80	17 05.3	+54.47
22	ζ	Dra	3.2	B6 III	. . . .	300	17 08.8	+65.71
23	β	Dra	2.8	G2 II	Rastaben	250	17 30.4	+52.30
25	ν	Dra	4.1	dA5 V	companion is 24 Dra	120	17 32.2	+55.18
26		Dra	5.2	dG1 V	. . . .	50	17 35.0	+61.87
31	ψ	Dra	4.3	dF6 IV	. . . .	70	17 41.9	+72.15
32	ξ	Dra	3.8	K2 III	Grumium	200	17 53.5	+56.87
33	γ	Dra	2.2	K5 III	Ettanin	100	17 56.6	+51.49
44	χ	Dra	3.6	F7 V	. . . .	25	18 21.1	+72.73
39		Dra	4.8	dA1 V	. . . .	150	18 23.9	+58.80
57	δ	Dra	3.1	G9 III	Altais	120	19 12.6	+67.66
63	ε	Dra	3.8	dG7 III	. . . .	150	19 48.2	+70.27

BINARY			Mag.		Spec.		PA	Sep.	Vis.
17		Dra	$5.^m4$	$6.^m4$	B9	A1	105°	3".3	tl
				5.5		B9	194	90	Op
21	μ	Dra	5.7	5.7	F7	F7 '90	24	1.9	tl
						2010	352	2.0	tl
25	ν	Dra	4.9	4.9	A5	A6	312	62	bn
26		Dra	5.3	8.0	G0	K3 '90	341	1.5	Tl
						2000	330	1.7	Tl
						2010	316	1.1	-
31	ψ	Dra	4.6	5.8	F5	F9	15	30.3	Bn
39		Dra	5.0	7.8	A1	A5	349	3.9	tl
				7.2		F6	21	89	bn
63	ε	Dra	3.9	7.3	G7	K5	21	3.2	tl

Comment on M102

Messier's logbook contains a galaxy close to NGC 5866 as his entry number 102. Yet his description suggests a double observation of M101. Did he make an error of 1^h in recording the right ascension? The designation M102 is thus ambiguous.

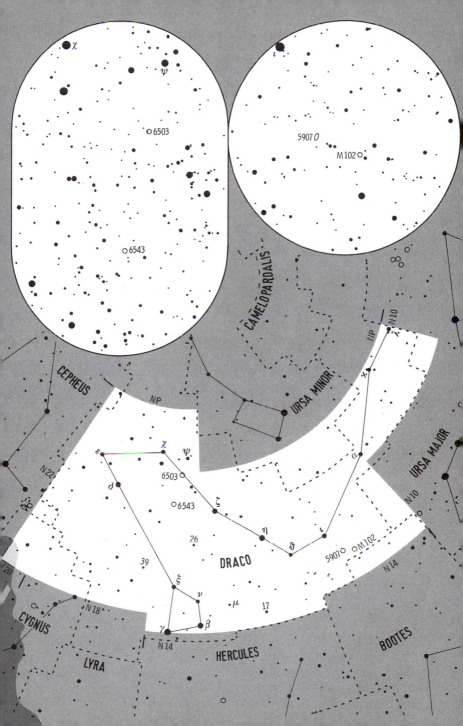

NEBULA		Const.	Mag.		Size	Shape	Type	Vis.	Dist.	R.A.	Dec.
6720	M57	Lyr	9^m	6$\frac{m}{(5')}$	1.5	R 3	Plan	Op	2000 ly	18^{h}53$\frac{1}{2}^m$	+33.0
6779	M56	Lyr	8½	8	5	X	Glob	bn	30 000	19 16½	+30.2
6826		Cyg	9	4	0.5	D 1	Plan	Op	3000	19 45	+50.5

6720 M57 **Ring Nebula,** the most famous planetary nebula, easy to find, looks almost like a star in binoculars, visible as a disk in small telescopes and as a nice oval ring in large telescopes, takes high magnification

6779 M56 dim globular cluster, hard to resolve into stars

6826 **Blinking Planetary,** in a telescope at high magnification the nebula is visible with averted vision, it disappears with direct vision while the 10½^m central star becomes visible

STAR			Mag.	Spec.	Name, Comments	Dist.	R.A.	Dec.
1	κ	Lyr	4.3	K2 III	. . . .	250 ly	18^{h}19^m.9	+36.06
3	α	Lyr	0.0	A0 V	**Vega**	25	18 36.9	+38.78
4,5	ε	Lyr	3.9	d A7 V	The Double Double .	150	18 44.4	+39.64
6,7	ζ	Lyr	4.1	d A4 IV	. . . .	200	18 44.8	+37.60
10	β	Lyr	3.3–4.3	d B7 V	Sheliak	300	18 50.1	+33.36
12	δ²	Lyr	4.3	M4 II	. . . .	800	18 54.5	+36.90
13		Lyr	3.9–5.0	M5 III	R Lyrae	250	18 55.3	+43.95
14	γ	Lyr	3.2	B9 III	Sulaphat	200	18 58.9	+32.69
1	κ	Cyg	3.8	K0 III	. . . .	150	19 17.1	+53.37
10	ι	Cyg	3.8	A5 V ·	. . . .	100	19 29.7	+51.73
6	β	Cyg	2.9	d G8 II	**Albireo**	400	19 30.7	+27.96
13	ϑ	Cyg	4.5	F 4 V	. . . .	60	19 36.4	+50.22
16		Cyg	5.3	d G3 V	. . . .	60	19 41.8	+50.52
18	δ	Cyg	2.9	d A0 IV	. . . .	150	19 45.0	+45.13
	χ	Cyg	3.3–14.2	K0 III	. . . .	100	19 50.6	+32.91
24	ψ	Cyg	4.9	d A4 IV	. . . .	200	19 55.6	+52.44
21	η	Cyg	3.9	K0 III	. . . .	200	19 56.3	+35.08

BINARY			Mag.	Spec.	PA	Sep.	Vis.
4,5	ε	Lyr	5.0 6.1	A4 F 1 '90	353°	2.6	tl
				2010	348	2.5	tl
			5.2 5.5	A8 F 0 '90	86	2.3	tl
				2010	78	2.4	tl
				both pairs	173	209	Ey
6,7	ζ	Lyr	4.4 5.7	A3 F 0	150	43.7	Bn
10	β	Lyr	3–4 7.2	B7 B 7	149	45.7	Bn
6	β	Cyg	3.1 5.1	K3!B 8	54	34.5	Bn
16		Cyg	6.0 6.2	G2 G4	134	39.6	bn
18	δ	Cyg	2.9 6.3	B9 F 1 '90	227	2.4	Tl
				2010	217	2.6	Tl
24	ψ	Cyg	4.9 7.4	A3 F 4	176	3.2	tl

VARIABLE STAR

10 β Lyr	β **Lyrae**
Period	12.93 d
Min.	2447903
secondary mini-	
mum magnit.	3.8

13 R Lyr semiregular
Period ≈ 46 d

χ Cyg	Mira type
Period	407 d
Max.	2448250
Min.	phase 0.59
Amplitude	10.9 !

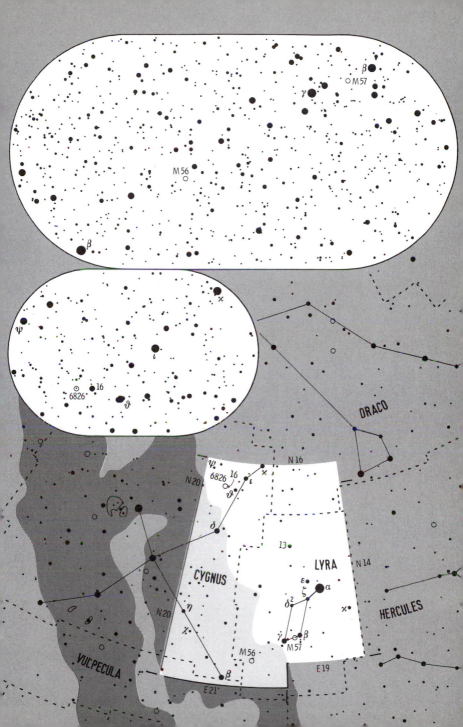

NEBULA		Const.	Mag.		Size	Shape	Type	Vis.	Dist.	R.A.	Dec.
6913	M29	Cyg	7^m	$7\frac{m}{(5')}$	$6'$	p n	Open	op	4000 ly	20^h24^m	$+38.5$
6940		Vul	7	10	25	m	Open	op	2500	20 35	+28.3
6960		Cyg	9	12	60	Fi 9	Diff	tl	1500	20 46	+30.7
IC 5067		Cyg	7	12	60	Em2	Diff	bn	4000	20 50	+44.0
6992		Cyg	8	12	60	Fi 7	Diff	Bn	1500	20 57	+31.4
7000		Cyg	5	11	120	Em2	Diff	Ey	4000	20 59	+44.3
7027		Cyg	9	3	0.3	A 4	Plan	Op	3000	21 07	+42.2

6913 M29	only a few stars in rich field, inconspicuous at too high power
6940	large nebulous patch in binoculars, nicely resolved in a telescope
6960	**Veil Nebula, Cirrus Nebula, Filamentary Nebula**, dim filaments on both sides of the foreground star 52 Cygni, see also NGC 6992
IC 5067	**Pelican Nebula**, invisible except at lowest magnification, distinct only through a nebular filter, test object for dark sky
6992	**Veil Nebula, Cirrus Nebula, Network Nebula**, supernova remnant, very dark sky and lowest magnification essential, impressive filaments visible when using a nebular filter (NGC 6992–6995)
7000	**North America Nebula**, easier to find with unaided eye than with a telescope, nebular filter very helpful, region with highest contrast is "Mexico", northern part merges into Milky Way
7027	easily visible as a star, only at very high magnification as a disk

STAR			Mag.	Spec.	Name, Comments	Dist.	R.A.	Dec.
31	o^1	Cyg	3.8	d K0 II	. . . .	500 ly	$20^h13.6$	$+46.74$
29		Cyg	4.8	d A7 V	. . . .	120	20 14.6	+36.80
32	o^2	Cyg	4.0	K3 Ib	. . . .	1000	20 15.5	+47.71
34		Cyg	3.0–6.0	B2 Ia	P Cygni	5000	20 17.8	+38.03
37	γ	Cyg	2.2	F8 Ib	Sadr	800	20 22.2	+40.26
41		Cyg	4.0	F5 II	. . . .	500	20 29.4	+30.37
46	ω^2	Cyg	5.1	d K2 III	. . . .	500	20 31.2	+49.22
50	α	Cyg	1.3	A2 Ia	**Deneb**	2000	20 41.4	+45.28
52		Cyg	4.2	K0 III	. . . .	200	20 45.7	+30.72
53	ε	Cyg	2.5	K0 III	. . . .	70	20 46.2	+33.97
54	λ	Cyg	4.5	d B5 V	. . . .	600	20 47.4	+36.49
T		Vul	5.4–6.1	F5 Ib	. . . .	3000	20 51.5	+28.25
58	ν	Cyg	3.9	A0 V	. . . .	150	20 57.2	+41.17
62	ξ	Cyg	3.7	K5 Ib	. . . .	1000	21 04.9	+43.93
64	ζ	Cyg	3.2	G8 III	. . . . : . .	200	21 12.9	+30.23

BINARY			Mag.	Spec.	PA	Sep.	Vis.
31	o^1	Cyg	3.8 7.0	K2!B6	$173°$	$107''$	bn
29		Cyg	5.0 6.6	A2!K0	153	212	Op
46	ω^2	Cyg	5.4 6.6	M2!A0	265	256	op
54	λ	Cyg	4.9 6.1	B5 B7 '90	11	0.9	Tl
				2010	2	0.9	Tl

VARIABLE STAR	
34 P Cyg	irregular
T Vul	Cepheid
Period	4.4355 d
Max.	2447893.0
Min.	phase 0.69

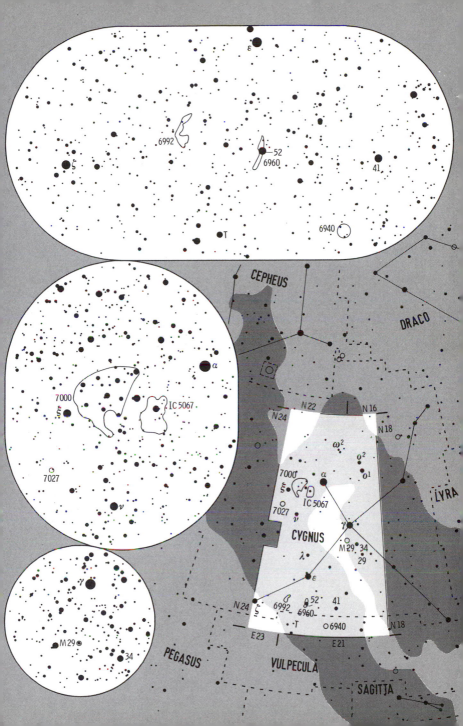

NEBULA	Const.	Mag.		Size	Shape	Type	Vis.	Dist.	R.A.	Dec.
6939	Cep	9^m	$10^m_{(5')}$	$8'$	m	Open	bn	6000 ly	20^h31^m	$+60°6$
6946	Cep	9	11	10	Sc 1	Galx	Bn	15 M	20 35	+60.2
IC 1396	Cep	4	9	50	m n	Open	ey	2000	21 39	+57.5
7654 M52	Cas	$7\frac{1}{2}$	9	12	r	Open	Op	5000	23 24	+61.6
7789	Cas	7	9	15	r	Open	op	6000	23 57	+56.7

6939	faint open cluster, very hard to resolve into stars
6946	difficult object, galaxy without central core or other features
IC 1396	sparse, inconspicuous in a telescope, better in opera glasses, surrounding diffuse nebula (dashed) visible with nebula filter
7654 M52	nebulous in binoculars, many faint stars in a telescope
7789	enormous number of stars for an open cluster, nebulous background only well resolved into stars in a large telescope

STAR			Mag.	Spec.	Name, Comments	Dist.	R.A.	Dec.
3	η	Cep	3^m4	K0 IV	. . . .	45 ly	20^h45^m3	$+61°84$
T		Cep	5.3–11.2	M7 III	. . . .	1000	21 09.5	+68.49
5	α	Cep	2.4	A7 V	Alderamin	45	21 18.6	+62.59
8	β	Cep	3.2	d B1 IV	Alfirk	800	21 28.7	+70.56
	μ	Cep	3.4–5.1	M2 Ia	. . . .	3000	21 43.5	+58.78
17	ξ	Cep	4.3	d A5 V	. . . .	120	22 03.8	+64.63
21	ζ	Cep	3.4	K1 Ib	. . . .	800	22 10.9	+58.20
23	ϵ	Cep	4.2	F0 IV	. . . .	100	22 15.0	+57.04
27	δ	Cep	3.4–4.2	d F6 Ib	. . . .	1200	22 29.2	+58.42
32	ι	Cep	3.5	K1 III	. . . .	120	22 49.7	+66.20
33	π	Cep	4.4	d G2 III	. . . .	200	23 07.9	+75.39
34	o	Cep	4.7	d G9 III	. . . .	150	23 18.6	+68.11
4		Cas	4.9	d M0 III	. . . .	300	23 24.8	+62.28
AR		Cas	4.8	d B4 V	. . . .	600	23 30.0	+58.55
35	γ	Cep	3.2	K1 IV	Errai	50	23 39.3	+77.63
7	ϱ	Cas	4.1–6.2	G2 Ia	. . . .	8000	23 54.4	+57.50
8	σ	Cas	4.9	d B1 IV	. . . .	1500	23 59.0	+55.76

BINARY			Mag.	Spec.	PA	Sep.	Vis.
8	β	Cep	3^m2 7^m8	B1 A2	$249°$	$13''3$	tl
17	ξ	Cep	4.5 6.5	A3 F7 '90	275	8.1	tl
				2010	274	8.3	tl
27	δ	Cep	3–4 6.3	F8! B7	191	41.0	Bn
33	π	Cep	4.6 6.6	G3 F3 '90	346	1.2	Tl
				2010	6	1.2	Tl
34	o	Cep	4.9 7.1	K0 F6 '90	220	2.9	tl
				2010	226	2.7	tl
4		Cas	5.0 7.5	M0 K	226	99	bn
AR		Cas	4.9 6.9	B3 A0	269	76	bn
8	σ	Cas	5.0 7.1	B1 B3	326	3.0	tl

VARIABLE STAR

T Cep	Mira type
Period	390 d
Max.	2448073
μ Cep	semiregular
Period	≈ 730 d
27 δ Cep	**Cepheid**
Period	5.36634 d
Max.	2447897.49
Min.	phase 0.75
7 ϱ Cas	semiregular
Period	100–1000 d

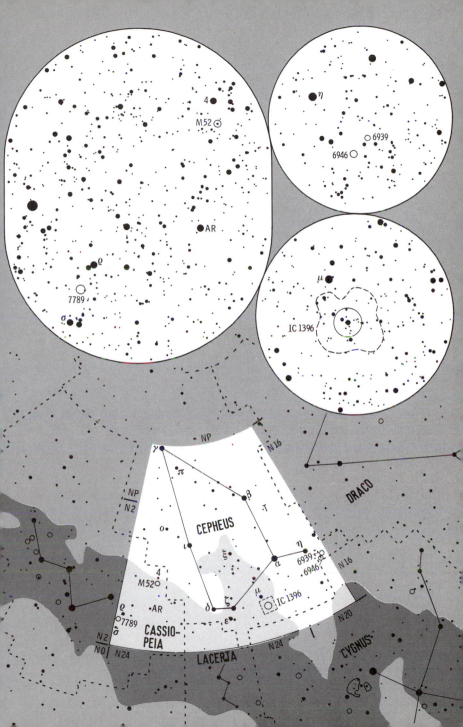

NEBULA		Const.	Mag.		Size	Shape	Type	Vis.	Dist.	R.A.	Dec.
7092	M39	Cyg	5^m	$9^m_{(5')}$	$30'$	p	Open	Ey	800 ly	21^h32^m	$+48°.4$
7209		Lac	7	10	20	m	Open	op	3 000	22 05	$+46.5$
7243		Lac	$6\frac{1}{2}$	9	20	p	Open	op	3 000	22 15	$+49.9$
7662		And	9	4	0.5	R 1	Plan	Op	3 000	23 26	$+42.5$

7092	M39	consists of a few bright stars which are well resolved in binoculars, rather disappointing view in a telescope
7209		binoculars show few stars within a nebulous background, which resolves into stars only in a telescope
7243		partially resolved already in binoculars, irregular shape, a telescope does not show much more
7662		**Blue Snowball**, visible in binoculars as a star, higher power reveals a nebulous disk, in large telescopes the ring with somewhat darker center becomes visible, distinctly greenish

STAR		Mag.	Spec.	Name, Comments	Dist.	R.A.	Dec.
61	Cyg	$4^m.8$	d K6 V	Piazzi's Flying Star,	11 ly	$21^h06^m.9$	$+38°.75$
65 τ	Cyg	3.7	F 1 IV	⌊motion 5".2 per year⌋	70	21 14.8	$+38.05$
67 σ	Cyg	4.2	B 9 Ia	. . . .	5 000	21 17.4	$+39.39$
73 ϱ	Cyg	4.0	G8 III	. . . .	200	21 34.0	$+45.59$
W	Cyg	5.4–6.2 ·	M5 III	. . . .	500	21 36.0	$+45.37$
79	Cyg	5.3	d A0 V	. . . .	400	21 43.5	$+38.29$
78 μ	Cyg	4.4	d F 7 V	. . . .	60	21 44.1	$+28.74$
81 π^2	Cyg	4.2	B 3 III	. . . .	800	21 46.8	$+49.31$
1	Lac	4.1	K3 II	. . . .	300	22 16.0	$+37.75$
2	Lac	4.6	B 6 V	. . . .	400	22 21.0	$+46.54$
3 β	Lac	4.4	G9 III	. . . .	150	22 23.6	$+52.23$
4	Lac	4.6	B 9 Ia	. . . .	5 000	22 24.5	$+49.48$
5	Lac	4.4	M0 II	. . . .	800	22 29.5	$+47.71$
7· α	Lac	3.8	A 2 V	. . . .	100	22 31.3	$+50.28$
8	Lac	5.3	d B 2 V	. . . .	2 000	22 35.9	$+39.63$
1 o	And	3.7	B 6 III	. . . .	300	23 01.9	$+42.33$
16 λ	And	3.7–4.0	G8 III	. . . .	70	23 37.6	$+46.46$
17 ι	And	4.3	B 8 V	. . . .	250	23 38.1	$+43.27$
19 κ	And	4.1	B 9 IV	. . . .	250	23 40.4	$+44.33$

BINARY		Mag.		Spec.		PA	Sep.	Vis.
61	· Cyg	$5^m.2$	$6^m.0$	K5	K7 '90	$148°$	$29".7$	Bn
					2010	152	30.8	Bn
79	Cyg	5.6	6.9	A0	A0	61	150	Op
78 μ	Cyg	4.8	6.1	F 6	G2 '90	307	1.5	Tl
					2000	320	1.2	Tl
					2010	343	0.9	Tl
			6.9		A 5	47	194	Op
8	Lac	5.7	6.5	B 2	B 2	186	22.4	Bn

VARIABLE STAR

W Cyg	semiregular
Period	≈ 126 d
Max.	≈ 2448000
Min.	phase 0.50
period varies	
16 λ And	semiregular
Period	55 d
Max.	≈ 2447925

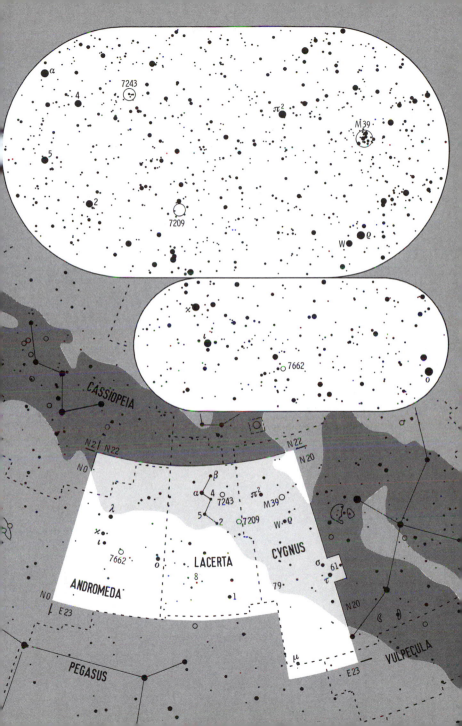

NEBULA		Const.	Mag.		Size	Shape	Type	Vis.	Dist.	R.A.	Dec.
247		Cet	9^m	$11\frac{m}{(5')}$	$20'$	Sd 7	Galx	Bn	8 Mly	0^h47^m	$-20°8$
253		Scl	7	9	25	Sc 7	Galx	op	8 M	0 48	-25.3
288		Scl	8	10	10	X	Glob	Op	30000	0 53	-26.6
1068	M77	Cet	9	8	4	Sb 2	Galx	bn	50 M	$2\ 42\frac{1}{2}$	0.0

247	large featureless galaxy, low power essential, difficult object
253	**Sculptor Galaxy**, fantastic galaxy, elongated in binoculars, dust features visible in large telescopes, small core
288	hard object among globulars, individual stars in large telescopes
1068　M77	bright Seyfert galaxy, active nucleus distinct at high power, binoculars show the nucleus well, but hardly anything else

STAR			Mag.	Spec.	Name, Comments	Dist.	R.A.	Dec.
	κ^1	Scl	5.4	d F 2 V	. . . .	100ly	0^h09^m3	$-27°99$
8	ι	Cet	3.6	K2 III	. . . .	200	0 19.4	$-\ 8.82$
T		Cet	5.0–6.9	M5 II	. . . .	2000	0 21.8	-20.06
16	β	Cet	2.0	K0 III	Diphda, Deneb Kaitos	70	0 43.6	-17.99
	α	Scl	4.3	B 8 III	. . . .	400	0 58.6	-29.36
31	η	Cet	3.5	K2 III	. . . .	120	1 08.6	-10.18
37		Cet	5.0	d F 3 V	. . . .	80	1 14.4	$-\ 7.92$
45	ϑ	Cet	3.6	K0 III	. . . .	120	1 24.0	$-\ 8.18$
	τ	Scl	5.7	d F 2 V	. . . .	120	1 36.1	-29.91
52	τ	Cet	3.5	G8 V	. . . .	12	1 44.1	-15.94
53	χ	Cet	4.5	d F 3 IV	. . . .	100	1 49.6	-10.69
55	ζ	Cet	3.7	K1 III	Baten Kaitos . . .	200	1 51.5	-10.34
59	υ	Cet	4.0	M1 III	. . . .	250	2 00.0	-21.08
66		Cet	5.5	d F 9 V	. . . .	70	2 12.8	$-\ 2.39$
68	o	Cet	2.0–10.1	M7 III	**Mira**	100	2 19.3	$-\ 2.98$
73	ξ^2	Cet	4.3	B 9 III	. . . .	300	2 28.2	$+\ 8.46$
	ω	For	4.9	d B 9 V	. . . .	300	2 33.8	-28.23
82	δ	Cet	4.1	B 2 IV	. . . .	800	2 39.5	$+\ 0.33$
86	γ	Cet	3.5	d A 3 V	. . . .	80	2 43.3	$+\ 3.24$
89	π	Cet	4.3	B 7 V	. . . .	300	2 44.1	-13.86
87	μ	Cet	4.3	F 0 IV	. . . .	100	2 44.9	$+10.11$
92	α	Cet	2.5	M2 III	Menkar	150	3 02.3	$+\ 4.09$

BINARY			Mag.		Spec.		PA	Sep.	Vis.
	κ^1	Scl	6.1	6.2	F 2	F 2	$261°$	1.7	tl
37		Cet	5.1	7.9	F 3	G7	331	49.7	Bn
	τ	Scl	6.0	7.1	F 1	F 7 '90	335	1.9	tl
						2010	340	2.5	tl
53	χ	Cet	4.7	6.8	F 2	G1	250	184	Op
66		Cet	5.7	7.6	F 8	G4	234	16.5	tl
	ω	For	5.0	7.7	B 9	A 7	245	10.8	tl
86	γ	Cet	3.5	7.3	A 2!	G5	296	2.8	Tl

VARIABLE STAR

T Cet	semiregular
Period	159 d
Max.	≈ 2448030
68 o Cet	**Mira**
Period	331.9 d
Max.	2448159
Min.	phase 0.62
Mean	$3.4–9.1$

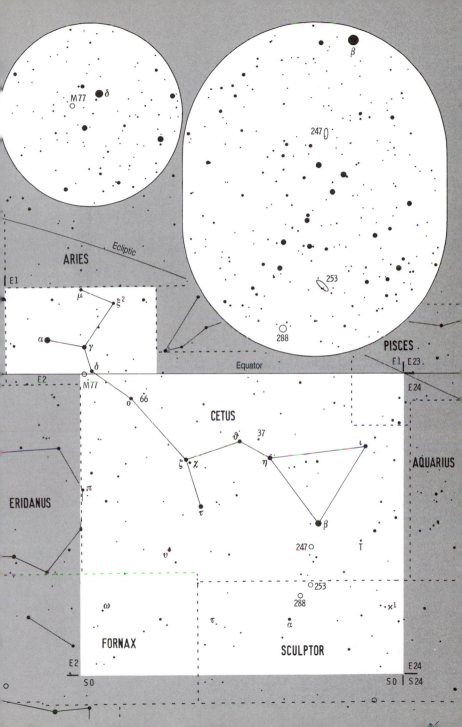

M77

δ

ARIES

Ecliptic

247

253

288

PISCES

E1

E2

μ

ξ²

α

γ

δ

M77

o 66

Equator

CETUS

ϑ

37

ζ χ

η

ι

E1 E23

E24

AQUARIUS

ERIDANUS

π

τ

β

v

247

T

253

288

ω

x¹

FORNAX

τ

α

SCULPTOR

E2

S0

E24

S0 S24

NEBULA	Const.	Mag.	Size	Shape	Type	Vis.	Dist.	R.A.	Dec.
628 M74	Psc	$9\frac{1}{2}^m 11^m_{(5')}$	8'	Sc 1	Galx	Bn	30 M ly	1^h37^m	$+15.8$

628   M74   very difficult except under darkest sky, lowest magnification

STAR			Mag.	Spec.	Name, Comments		Dist.	R.A.	Dec.
88	γ	Peg	2.8	B 2 IV	**Algenib**		500 ly	$0^h13^m.2$	$+15°.18$
35		Psc	5.8	d F 0 V	. . . .		150	0 15.0	+ 8.82
47		Psc	4.7–5.4	M3 III	TV Piscium		400	0 28.0	+17.89
34	ζ	And	4.0	K1 III	. . . .		150	0 47.3	+24.27
63	δ	Psc	4.4	K5 III	. . . .		300	0 48.7	+ 7.59
65		Psc	5.5	d F 2 IV	. . . .		250	0 49.9	+27.71
36		And	5.5	d K1 IV	. . . .		200	0 55.0	+23.63
71	ε	Psc	4.3	K0 III	. . . .		200	1 02.9	+ 7.89
74	ψ¹	Psc	4.7	d A1 IV	. . . .		400	1 05.7	+21.47
86	ζ	Psc	4.9	d A8 IV	. . . .		150	1 13.7	+ 7.58
99	η	Psc	3.6	G8 III	. . . .		150	1 31.5	+15.35
106	ν	Psc	4.4	K3 III	. . . .		150	1 41.4	+ 5.49
110	o	Psc	4.3	G9 III	. . . .		200	1 45.4	+ 9.16
1		Ari	5.9	d G5 III	. . . .		250	1 50.1	+22.28
5	γ	Ari	3.9	d A0 V	Mesarthim		150	1 53.5	+19.29
111	ξ	Psc	4.6	K0 III	. . . .		250	1 53.6	+ 3.19
6	β	Ari	2.6	A5 V	Sheratan		45	1 54.6	+20.81
9	λ	Ari	4.7	d F1 IV	. . . .		150	1 57.9	+23.60
113	α	Psc	3.8	d A1 V	. . . .		150	2 02.0	+ 2.76
10		Ari	5.6	d F 7 IV	. . . .		120	2 03.7	+25.94
13	α	Ari	2.0	K2 III	**Hamal**		80	2 07.2	+23.46
41		Ari	3.6	B 8 V	. . . .		120	2 50.0	+27.26
48	ε	Ari	4.6	d A2 V	. . . .		200	2 59.2	+21.34

BINARY		Mag.	Spec.	PA	Sep.	Vis.
35	Psc	6.0 7.7	F 0 A 7	148°	11.6	tl
65	Psc	6.3 6.3	F 2 F 3	297	4.4	tl
36	And	6.0 6.4	K1 K '90	292	0.8	Tl
			2000	313	0.9	Tl
			2010	327	1.1	Tl
74	ψ¹ Psc	5.3 5.6	A1 A0	159	30.0	Bn
86	ζ Psc	5.2 6.3	A8 F7	63	22.9	Bn
1	Ari	6.2 7.4	K1!A6	165	2.8	tl
5	γ Ari	4.6 4.7	B9 A1	0	7.7	tl
9	λ Ari	4.8 7.3	F 0 G0	46	37.4	Bn
113	α Psc	4.2 5.2	A1 A3 '90	278	1.9	tl
			2010	265	1.8	tl
10	Ari	5.9 7.3	F 7 F8 '90	331	1.1	Tl
			2010	345	1.4	Tl
48	ε Ari	5.2 5.5	A2 A2	211	1.4	Tl

VARIABLE STAR

47 TV Psc semiregular
    Period   50–85 d

Comment on M74:
Some amateurs want
to observe all 110
Messier objects dur-
ing just one night in
March. M74 is then
the most difficult ob-
ject right after sun-
set, and M30 the most
difficult before sunrise.
Advice: it is better
to take your time.

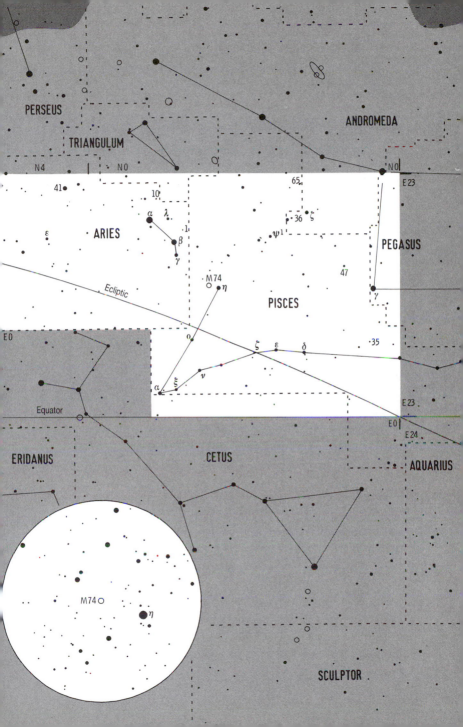

NEBULA	Const.	Mag.		Size	Shape	Type	Vis.	Dist.	R.A.	Dec.
1360	For	8^m	8$\frac{m}{(5')}$	6$'$	D 3	Plan	Op	1000 ly	3^{h}33^m	−25$°$8
1535	Eri	10	4	0.3	D 2	Plan	bn	5000	4 14	−12.7

1360	bright large planetary, though it is not well known among observers, fine object for binoculars, 11^m central star is hard to see, it is extremely hot, surface temperature ≈ 100 000 K
1535	stellar in binoculars, light features in large telescopes at high magnification, nebula contains faint 12^m central star

STAR		Mag.	Spec.	Name, Comments	Dist.	R.A.	Dec.
1	τ^1 Eri	4^{m}5	F 6 V	. . . .	50 ly	2^{h}45^{m}1	−18$°$57
	β For	4.5	G7 III	. . . .	200	2 49.1	−32.41
3	η Eri	3.9	K1 III	. . . .	100	2 56.4	− 8.90
11	τ^3 Eri	4.1	A5 V	. . . .	80	3 02.4	−23.62
	α For	3.9	d F 8 IV	. . . .	50	3 12.1	−28.99
16	τ^4 Eri	3.6	M3 III	. . . .	250	3 19.5	−21.76
18	ε Eri	3.7	K2 V	. . . .	11	3 32.9	− 9.46
19	τ^5 Eri	4.3	B8 V	. . . .	300	3 33.8	−21.63
23	δ Eri	3.5	K0 IV	. . . .	30	3 43.2	− 9.76
27	τ^6 Eri	4.2	F3 V	. . . .	60	3 46.8	−23.25
32	Eri	4.5	d G2 III	. . . .	250	3 54.3	− 2.95
34	γ Eri	3.0	M0 III	Zaurak	150	3 58.0	−13.51
38	o^1 Eri	4.0	F 2 III	. . . .	200	4 11.9	− 6.84
39	Eri	4.8	d K3 III	. . . .	300	4 14.4	−10.26
40	o^2 Eri	4.4	d K1 V	. . . .	16	4 15.3	− 7.65
41	υ^4 Eri	3.6	B8 V	. . . .	120	4 17.9	−33.80
43	υ^3 Eri	4.0	K5 III	. . . .	250	4 24.0	−34.02
52	υ^2 Eri	3.8	G9 III	. . . .	200	4 35.6	−30.56
48	ν Eri	3.9	B 2 III	. . . .	1000	4 36.3	− 3.35
53	Eri	3.9	K2 III	. . . .	150	4 38.2	−14.30
57	μ Eri	4.0	B 5 IV	. . . .	400	4 45.5	− 3.25
67	β Eri	2.8	A3 III	Cursa	90	5 07.8	− 5.09
	ε Col	3.9	K1 III	. . . .	150	5 31.2	−35.47
	α Col	2.6	B7 IV	Phact	150	5 39.6	−34.07
	β Col	3.1	K2 III	. . . .	150	5 51.0	−35.77
	γ Col	4.4	B3 IV	. . . .	800	5 57.5	−35.28
	δ Col	3.9	G4 III	. . . .	120	6 22.1	−33.44

BINARY		Mag.	Spec.	PA	Sep.	Vis.
	α For	4^{m}0 6^{m}5	F 7 G7 '90	298$°$	4$''$5	tl
			2000	299	5.1	tl
			2010	300	5.5	tl
32	Eri	4.8 6.1	G8!A2	347	6.8	tl
39	Eri	4.9 8.0	K3 G2	144	6.4	tl
40	o^2 Eri	4.4 9.5	K1!A2	103	83	Bn

Comment on o^2 Eri

Its companion is the most easily observable white dwarf. Its diameter measures only 20 000 km = 12 000 miles.

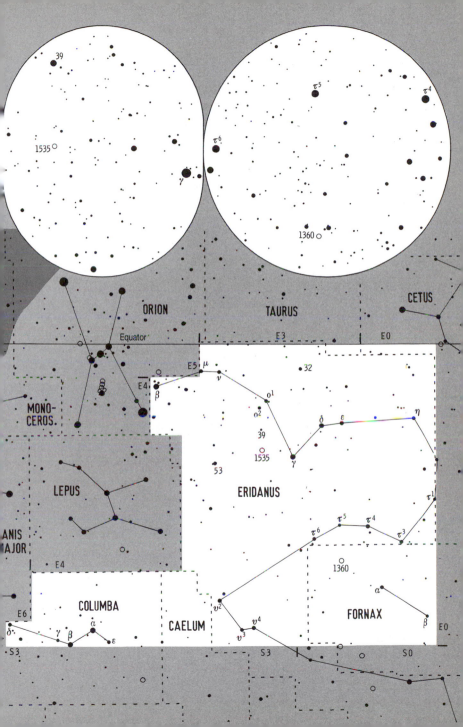

NEBULA	Const.	Mag.		Size	Shape	Type	Vis.	Dist.	R.A.	Dec.
M45	Tau	1½ᵐ	8ᵐ(5')	100'	r n	Open	ey	400ly	3ʰ47ᵐ	+24°.1
Hyades	Tau	0½	9	300	m	Open	ey	150	4 28	+16.7
1647	Tau	6½	11	40	m	Open	op	2500	4 46	+19.1
1952 M1	Tau	9	9	6	Fi 4	Diff	bn	4000	5 34½	+22.0

M45		**Pleiades, Seven Sisters**, marvelous with unaided eye or binoculars, dim reflection nebulae under darkest sky
Hyades		only impressive with unaided eye or opera glasses, scattered stars, closest open cluster, Aldebaran is foreground star
1647		large open cluster, resolved into many stars in binoculars
1952	M1	**Crab Nebula**, difficult in binoculars, elongated, irregular in large telescopes, remnant of the supernova in 1054

STAR			Mag.	Spec.	Name, Comments	Dist.	R.A.	Dec.
1	o	Tau	3ᵐ6	G7 III	. . . .	150ly	3ʰ24ᵐ8	+ 9°03
2	ξ	Tau	3.7	B9 V	. . . .	150	3 27.2	+ 9.73
17		Tau	3.7	B6 III	Electra, in M45 . .	400	3 44.9	+24.11
19		Tau	4.3	B6 IV	Taygeta, in M45 . .	400	3 45.2	+24.47
20		Tau	3.9	B7 III	Maia, in M45 . . .	400	3 45.8	+24.37
23		Tau	4.2	B6 IV	Merope, in M45 . .	400	3 46.3	+23.95
25	η	Tau	2.8	B7 III	Alcyone, in M45 . .	400	3 47.5	+24.11
27		Tau	3.6	B8 III	Atlas, in M45 . . .	400	3 49.2	+24.05
28		Tau	4.8–5.5	B8 V	Pleione, BU Tau, in M45	400	3 49.2	+24.47
35	λ	Tau	3.4–3.9	B3 V	. . . .	300	4 00.7	+12.49
38	ν	Tau	3.9	A1 V	. . . .	100	4 03.2	+ 5.99
47		Tau	4.8	d G5 III	. . . .	200	4 13.9	+ 9.26
54	γ	Tau	3.6	K0 III	in Hyades	150	4 19.8	+15.63
61	δ¹	Tau	3.8	K0 III	in Hyades	150	4 22.9	+17.54
68	δ³	Tau	4.3	d A2 V	in Hyades	150	4 25.5	+17.93
74	ε	Tau	3.5	K0 III	in Hyades	150	4 28.6	+19.18
77	ϑ¹	Tau	3.8	K0 III	in Hyades } Sep. 5'.7	150	4 28.6	+15.96
78	ϑ²	Tau	3.4	A7 III	in Hyades }	150	4 28.7	+15.87
88		Tau	4.2	d A4 V	. . . .	80	4 35.7	+10.16
87	α	Tau	0.9	K5 III	**Aldebaran**	60	4 35.9	+16.51
94	τ	Tau	4.2	d B3 V	. . . .	600	4 42.2	+22.96
112	β	Tau	1.7	B7 III	**Elnath, Nath** . . .	120	5 26.3	+28.61
118		Tau	5.4	d B8 V	. . . .	400	5 29.3	+25.15
123	ζ	Tau	3.0	B3 III	. . . .	500	5 37.6	+21.14

BINARY		Mag.		Spec.		PA	Sep.	Vis.
47	Tau	4ᵐ9	7ᵐ3	G5	G	348°	1"2	Tl
68	δ³ Tau	4.3	7.6	A1	G0	350	1.6	Tl
88	Tau	4.3	7.8	A4	F8	299	70	Bn
94	τ Tau	4.3	7.2	B3	A0	213	63	Bn
118	Tau	5.8	6.6	B8	A0	207	4.8	tl

VARIABLE STAR

28 BU Tau   irregular
35 λ Tau   Algol type
   Period   3.95295 d
   Min.   2447892.82
   Max. ph.0.07–0.93

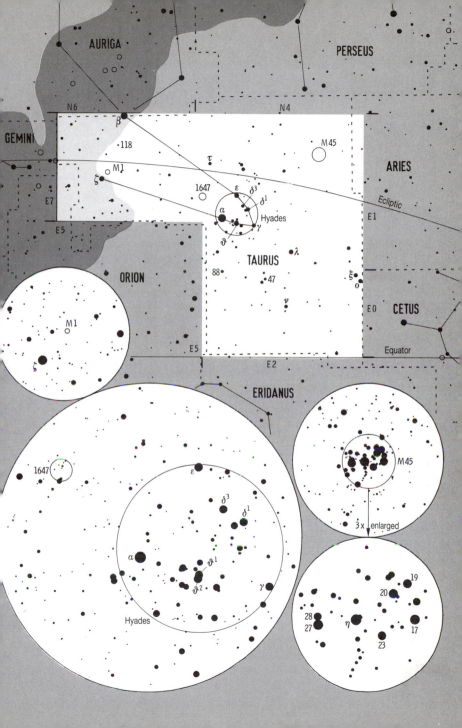

NEBULA	Const.	Mag.		Size	Shape	Type	Vis.	Dist.	R.A.	Dec.
1904 M79	Lep	8^m	9$\frac{m}{(5')}$	8$'$	V	Glob	Op	40 000 ly	5^{h}24$\frac{1}{2}^m$	−24°5
1981	Ori	5	8	25	p n	Open	Ey	1 500	5 35	− 4.4
1973	Ori	9	11	20	Re 3	Diff	Bn	1 500	5 35	− 4.8
1976 M42	Ori	4	8	40	Em3	Diff	ey	1 500	5 36	− 5.4
1982 M43	Ori	9	10	12	Em3	Diff	bn	1 500	5 36	− 5.3

1904 M79 very difficult to resolve, far outside our galaxy
1981 only a few bright stars, hard to recognize as a cluster
1973 dim object, the three sections are NGC 1973, 1975, 1977
1976 M42 **Orion Nebula**, primary nebula of all diffuse nebulae, impressive in every scope, dust clouds, bright arcs, and embedded stars are fantastic, to an experienced observer a large telescope can show more detail than impressive photographs
1982 M43 northern part of the Orion Nebula, separated by a dust cloud

STAR		Const.	Mag.	Spec.	Name, Comments	Dist.	R.A.	Dec.
R		Lep	5.5–11.7	C6 II	. . . .	3 000 ly	4^{h}59^{m}6	−14°81
2	ε	Lep	3.2	K5 III		150	5 05.5	−22.37
RX		Lep	5.0–7.0	M5 III		500	5 11.4	−11.85
5	μ	Lep	3.0–3.4	B 9 III	. . . .	200	5 12.9	−16.21
4	κ	Lep	4.4	d B9 V	. . . .	250	5 13.2	−12.94
19	β	Ori	0.1	d B8 Ia	**Rigel**	1 000	5 14.5	− 8.20
20	τ	Ori	3.6	B 5 III	. . . .	400	5 17.6	− 6.84
9	β	Lep	2.8	G4 II	Nihal	300	5 28.2	−20.76
11	α	Lep	2.6	F 0 Ib	Arneb . ⌈is 43 Ori⌉	1 000	5 32.7	−17.82
41	ϑ	Ori	4.0	d O8 V	Trapezium, companion	1 500	5 35.3	− 5.40
42		Ori	4.6	d B2 IV	in NGC 1973	1 500	5 35.4	− 4.84
44	ι	Ori	2.8	d O9 III	. . . .	1 500	5 35.4	− 5.91
13	γ	Lep	3.5	d F 7 V	. . . .	26	5 44.5	−22.45
14	ζ	Lep	3.6	A 3 V	. . . .	80	5 47.0	−14.82
53	κ	Ori	2.1	B 0 Ia	**Saiph**	1 500	5 47.8	− 9.67
15	δ	Lep	3.8	G8 III	. . . .	150	5 51.3	−20.88
16	η	Lep	3.7	F 0 IV	. . . .	70	5 56.4	−14.17

BINARY		Const.	Mag.		Spec.		PA	Sep.	Vis.
4	κ	Lep	4.4^m	7.3	B8	F 1	358°	2.6$''$	Tl
19	β	Ori	0.1	6.8	B8	B 7	202	9.5	Tl
41	ϑ	Ori	5.1	6.7	O6	O7	312	12.8	tl
				6.7		B 0	61	13.4	tl
				8.0		B 0	342	16.8	tl
			5.1	6.4	O9	B 0	92	52.5	bn
			both	5.1 stars			134	135	Op
42		Ori	4.7	7.9	B 2	B 7	213	1.6	Tl
44	ι	Ori	2.8	6.9	O9	B 7	141	11.3	tl
13	γ	Lep	3.6	6.2	F 6	G5	350	97	bn

VARIABLE STAR

R Lep	Mira type
Period	430 d
Max.	2448070
Min.	phase 0.45

reddish star, especially during minimum

RX Lep	irregular
5 μ Lep	irregular
Period	≈ 2 d

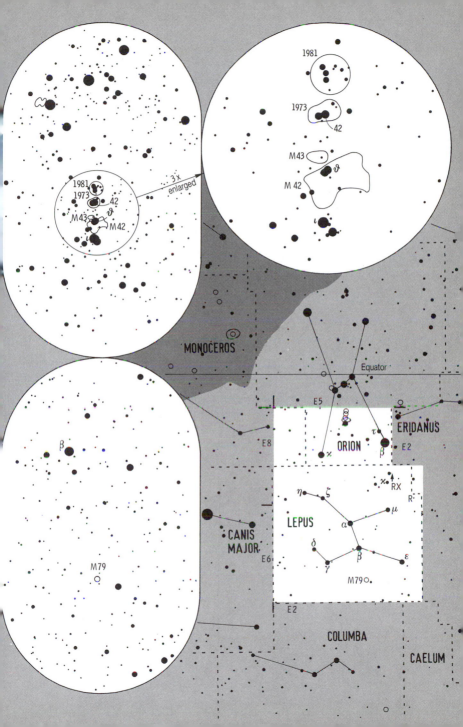

3 x enlarged

1981
1973
42
M43 ϑ
M42

1981
1973
42
M43
M42 ϑ
ι

β

M79

MONOCEROS

Equator

E5
E8

ORION
τ
β

ERIDANUS
E2

CANIS
MAJOR

E6

LEPUS

η ζ
α
μ
δ
β
γ
M79

x RX
R

ε

E2

COLUMBA

CAELUM

NEBULA	Const.	Mag.	Size	Shape	Type	Vis.	Dist.	R.A.	Dec.
1788	Ori	10^m $11^m_{(5')}$	$8'$	Re 4	Diff	tl	1500 ly	$5^h 07^m$	$- 3.4$
2024	Ori	8 11	20	Em2	Diff	Bn	1500	5 41	$- 1.9$
2068 M78	Ori	8 9	8	Re 3	Diff	Op	1500	5 47	$+ 0.1$

1788	one of the few reflection nebulae, very difficult, embedded star 10^m
2024	relatively bright and rich in features, but Alnitak outshines it, clean optics necessary, best if Alnitak is outside field of view
2068 M78	brightest reflection nebula, appears almost like a comet, dark dust features just visible in large telescopes, two embedded stars

STAR		Mag.	Spec.	Name, Comments	Dist.	R.A.	Dec.
1	π^3 Ori	$3^m_{.}2$	F 6 V	. . . .	25 ly	$4^h 49^m_{.}8$	$+ 6.96$
3	π^4 Ori	3.7	B 2 III	. . . .	1000	4 51.2	$+ 5.61$
8	π^5 Ori	3.7	B 2 III	. . . .	1000	4 54.3	$+ 2.44$
14	Ori	5.3	d A0 V	. . . .	150	5 07.9	$+ 8.50$
22	Ori	4.4	d B2 IV	. . . .	1500	5 21.7	$- 0.39$
23	Ori	4.9	d B1 V	. . . .	1500	5 22.8	$+ 3.55$
28	η Ori	3.4	d B1 V	. . . .	800	5 24.5	$- 2.40$
24	γ Ori	1.6	B 2 III	**Bellatrix**	400	5 25.1	$+ 6.35$
32	Ori	4.2	d B5 IV	. . . .	500	5 30.8	$+ 5.95$
33	Ori	5.5	d B1 V	. . . .	1500	5 31.2	$+ 3.29$
34	δ Ori	2.2	d O9 II	**Mintaka**	1500	5 32.0	$- 0.30$
VV	Ori	5.3–5.6	B 1 V	. . . .	1500	5 33.5	$- 1.16$
39	λ Ori	3.4	d O8 V	. . . .	1500	5 35.1	$+ 9.93$
46	ε Ori	1.7	B 0 Ia	**Alnilam**	1500	5 36.2	$- 1.20$
48	σ Ori	3.6	d B0 V	. . . .	1500	5 38.7	$- 2.60$
50	ζ Ori	1.8	d O9 Ib	**Alnitak**	1500	5 40.8	$- 1.94$
52	Ori	5.3	d A5 V	. . . .	200	5 48.0	$+ 6.45$
58	α Ori	0.4–1.3	M2 Ia	**Betelgeuse**	400	5 55.2	$+ 7.41$

BINARY		Mag.	Spec.	PA	Sep.	Vis.	VARIABLE STAR
14	Ori	$5^m_{.}8$ $6^m_{.}5$	A0 A	'90 349°	$0''_{.}7$	-	VV Ori β Lyrae type
				2000 322	0.8	Tl	Period 1.485378 d
				2010 301	0.9	Tl	Min. 2447892.59
22	Ori	4.7 5.7	B 2 B 3	240 242	op		Max. ph. ≈ 0.1–0.9
23	Ori	5.0 7.2	B 1 B 5	28 32.0	Bn		58 α Ori semiregular
28	η Ori	3.7 4.8	B 1 B 2	78 1.7	tl		Period ≈ 6 years
32	Ori	4.5 5.8	B 5 B 7	41 1.1	Tl		small variations
33	Ori	5.8 7.0	B 1 B 4	27 1.8	tl		with 200–400 d
34	δ Ori	2.2 6.9	O9 B 2	0 52.6	tl		period, fast drop
39	λ Ori	3.6 5.5	O8 B 0	43 4.4	tl		in brightness
48	σ Ori	3.8 6.6	B 0 B 2	84 12.9	tl		possible, brightest
		6.7	B 2	61 42.9	bn		variable star,
50	ζ Ori	1.9 4.0	O9 B 0	165 2.3	tl		no bright yellow
52	Ori	6.0 6.0	A1 F 0	214 1.4	Tl		comparison stars

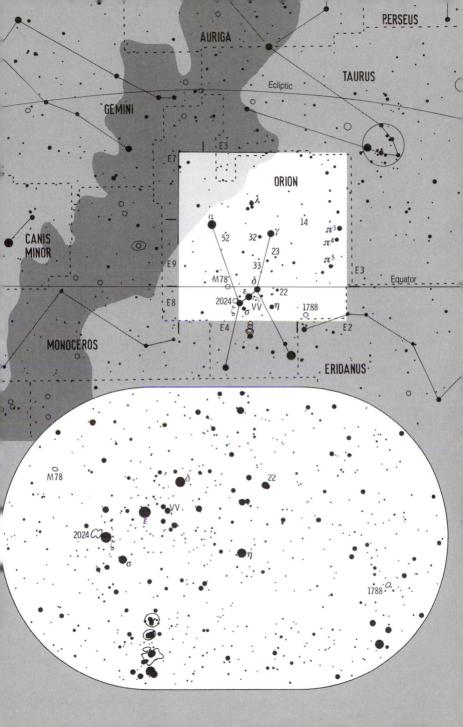

NEBULA	Const.	Mag.		Size	Shape	Type	Vis.	Dist.	R.A.	Dec.
2287 M41	CMa	5^m	9$\frac{m}{(5')}$	30'	m	Open	ey	2500 ly	6^{h}47^m	−20°.7
2362	CMa	4	5	6	p n	Open	ey	5000	7 19	−24.9
2447 M93	Pup	6½	9	15	m	Open	op	4000	7 45	−23.9

2287 M41	nicely resolved in binoculars, excellent object for small scopes, even visible with unaided eye as a glow, few faint stars, not too impressive in telescopes
2362	in binoculars essentially only one star is visible: τ CMa 4^m.4, well resolved in a small telescope, medium power is best
2447 M93	contains a few bright stars which are resolved in binoculars, while a nebulous background is caused by fainter stars, which are nicely resolved in telescopes, elongated shape

STAR		Mag.	Spec.	Name, Comments	Dist.	R.A.	Dec.
1	ζ CMa	3^m.0	d B 3 V	Phurud	300 ly	6^{h}20^m.3	−30°.06
2	β CMa	2.0	B 1 II	Mirzam	800	6 22.7	−17.96
7	ν² CMa	4.0	K 1 III	. . . .	80	6 36.7	−19.26
9	α CMa	−1.5	A 1 V	**Sirius**	8.7	6 45.1	−16.72
13	κ CMa	3.9	B 2 IV	. . . .	800	6 49.8	−32.51
16	o¹ CMa	3.8−4.0	K 3 Ia	. . . .	2000	6 54.1	−24.18
21	ε CMa	1.5	d B 2 II	**Adhara**	500	6 58.6	−28.97
22	σ CMa	3.5	K 8 Ib	. . . .	1500	7 01.7	−27.93
24	o² CMa	3.0	B 3 Ia	. . . .	2500	7 03.0	−23.83
23	γ CMa	4.1	B 8 II	. . . .	1000	7 03.8	−15.63
25	δ CMa	1.8	F 8 Ia	Wezen	3000	7 08.4	−26.39
27	CMa	4.4−4.7	B 3 III	EW Canis Majoris .	1000	7 14.3	−26.35
28	ω CMa	3.6−4.2	B 3 IV	. . . .	500	7 14.8	−26.77
145	CMa	4.5	d K 1 Ib	designation not general	2000	7 16.6	−23.32
29	CMa	4.8−5.3	O 8 Ia	UW Canis Majoris .	5000	7 18.7	−24.56
31	η CMa	2.4	d B 5 Ia	Aludra	2500	7 24.1	−29.30
n	Pup	5.1	d F 4 V	. . . .	120	7 34.3	−23.47
	κ Pup	3.8	d B 6 IV	also designated k Puppis	400	7 38.8	−26.80
3	Pup	4.0	A 2 Ia	. . . .	5000	7 43.8	−28.96
7	ξ Pup	3.2	d G 3 Ib	Aspidiske	800	7 49.3	−24.86
11	Pup	4.2	F 8 II	. . . .	400	7 56.9	−22.88
15	ϱ Pup	2.7	F 6 II	. . . .	300	8 07.5	−24.30

BINARY		Mag.	Spec.	PA	Sep.	Vis.
1	ζ CMa	3^m.0 7^m.6	B 3 ! K 0	338°	176″	bn
21	ε CMa	1.5 7.5	B 2 A 3	161	7.5	Tl
145	CMa	4.7 6.5	K 5 ! F 0	51	26.4	Bn
31	η CMa	2.4 7.0	B 5 A 0	285	180	bn
n	Pup	5.8 5.9	F 3 F 5	117	9.7	tl
	κ Pup	4.5 4.6	B 6 B 7	318	9.9	tl
7	ξ Pup	3.3 5.3	G 3 G 0	229	288	op

VARIABLE STAR

16 o¹ CMa	irregular	
27 EW CMa	irregular	
28 ω CMa	irregular	
	Period	≈ 1 d ?
29 UW CMa	β Lyr t.	
	Period	4.39341 d
	Min.	2447893.80

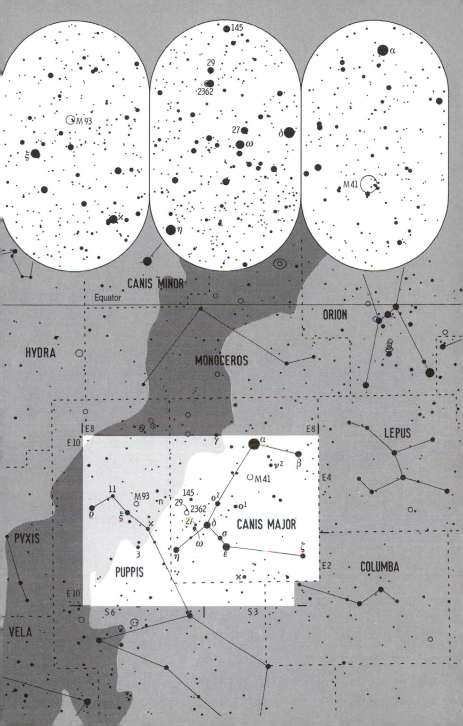

CANIS MINOR

Equator

ORION

HYDRA

MONOCEROS

LEPUS

E8

E10

E8

γ

α

β

ν²

M41

E4

11

M93

n

145

o²

o¹

ϱ

ξ

29

2362

ζ

χ

21

δ

CANIS MAJOR

PYXIS

3

ω

σ

η

ε

E2

COLUMBA

PUPPIS

χ

E10

S6

S3

VELA

M93

ξ

145

29

2362

27

ω

δ

M41

α

α

χ

η

M41

NEBULA	Const.	Mag.		Size	Shape	Type	Vis.	Dist.	R.A.	Dec.
2129		Gem	7^m $8^m_{(5')}$	$6'$	p	Open	op	6000ly	6^h01^m	$+23°3$
2168	M35	Gem	5½ 9	30	r	Open	ey	3000	6 09	+24.3
2175		Ori	7 10	20	p n	Open	op	6000	6 10	+20.3
2261		Mon	10 7	2	Re 5	Diff	Bn	3000	6 39	+ 8.7
2264		Mon	4 6	15	p n	Open	ey	3000	6 41	+ 9.9
2392		Gem	9 5	0.8	D 1	Plan	bn	2500	7 29	+20.9

2129		visible in binoculars, but very inconspicuous, very sparse
2168	M35	bright glow with some stars in binoculars, very nicely resolved in a telescope, impressive at low magnification
2175		very inconspicuous, dim diffuse nebula NGC 2174 on northern side
2261		**Hubble's Variable Nebula**, variable within days, detail visible with larger telescopes at high power
2264		**Christmas Tree**, elongated, one star 4^m7, others 8^m-10^m
2392		**Eskimo Nebula**, features need high magnification, bright center

STAR			Mag.	Spec.	Name, Comments	Dist.	R.A.	Dec.
7	η	Gem	3^m3-3^m9	M3 III	Tejat Prior	200ly	6^h14^m9	+22.51
13	μ	Gem	2.9	M3 III	Tejat Posterior . . .	150	6 23.0	+22.51
18	ν	Gem	4.1	B 7 IV	. . . .	300	6 29.0	+20.21
24	γ	Gem	1.9	A0 IV	**Alhena**	90	6 37.7	+16.40
15		Mon	4.7	d O7 V	in NGC 2264	3000	6 41.0	+ 9.90
27	ε	Gem	3.0	G8 Ib	Mebsuta	600	6 43.9	+25.13
31	ξ	Gem	3.4	F 5 III	. . . .	80	6 45.3	+12.90
34	ϑ	Gem	3.6	A3 III	. . . .	150	6 52.8	+33.96
38		Gem	4.7	d F 0 V	. . . .	80	6 54.6	+13.18
43	ζ	Gem	3.7–4.2	d G0 Ib	Mekbuda	1500	7 04.1	+20.57
54	λ	Gem	3.6	A3 V	. . . .	80	7 18.1	+16.54
55	δ	Gem	3.5	F 2 IV	Wasat	60	7 20.1	+21.98
60	ι	Gem	3.8	K0 III	. . . .	150	7 25.7	+27.80
62	ϱ	Gem	4.2	F 0 V	. . . .	60	7 29.1	+31.78
66	α	Gem	1.6	d A1 V	**Castor**	50	7 34.6	+31.89
69	υ	Gem	4.1	M0 III	. . . .	250	7 35.9	+26.90
77	κ	Gem	3.6	G8 III	. . . .	150	7 44.4	+24.40
78	β	Gem	1.1	K0 III	**Pollux**	35	7 45.3	+28.03

BINARY			Mag.		Spec.		PA	Sep.	Vis.
15		Mon	4^m7	7^m6	O7	B7	$214°$	$2''8$	Tl
38		Gem	4.7	7.7	A9	G5	145	7.1	tl
43	ζ	Gem	4	7.6	G0	G1	346	101	bn
66	α	Gem	1.9	2.9	A1	A2 '90	76	3.0	tl
						1995	69	3.5	tl
						2000	65	3.9	tl
						2005	61	4.3	tl
						2010	57	4.7	tl

VARIABLE STAR

7 η Gem	Algol type	
	Period	232.9 d
	Min.	2447973
	Max. ph.	.025–.975
43 ζ Gem	Cepheid	
	Period	10.1508 d
	Max.	2447896.68
	Min.	phase 0.50

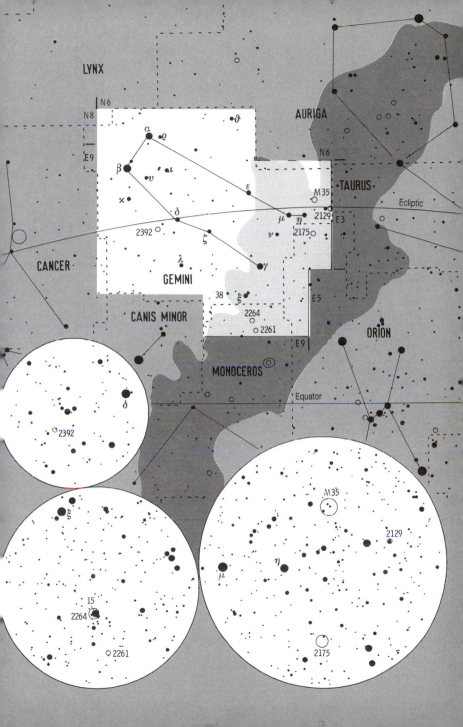

NEBULA	Const.	Mag.		Size	Shape	Type	Vis.	Dist.	R.A.	Dec.
2323 M50	Mon	7ᵐ	9ᵐ(5')	15'	r	Open	op	3000 ly	7ʰ03ᵐ	− 8°3
2360	CMa	8	10	12	m	Open	Op	5000	7 18	−15.6
2359	CMa	9	10	8	Em3	Diff	bn	4000	7 18	−13.2
2422 M47	Pup	4½	8	25	m	Open	ey	2000	7 37	−14.5
2423	Pup	7	10	20	m	Open	op	4000	7 37	−13.9
2437 M46	Pup	6½	10	25	r	Open	op	6000	7 42	−14.8
2438	Pup	11	8	1.0	R 0	Plan	tl	4000	7 42	−14.7
2539	Pup	8	11	20	m	Open	bn	5000	8 11	−12.8

2323	M50	brightest stars resolved in binoculars, leaves best impression in a telescope at low magnification, quite asymmetric
2360		a glow in binoculars, even in telescopes not completely resolved, distinct central condensation, asymmetric shape
2359		contains a few stars, diffuse nebula dim in binoculars, oval in telescopes, interesting detail visible with a nebular filter
2422	M47	impressive cluster in binoculars, no better in a telescope, visible with the unaided eye as a nebulous object
2423		consists of faint stars, some of which are binaries, quite symmetric distribution of stars, not resolved in binoculars
2437	M46	bright large glow in binoculars, impressive number of stars in larger telescopes, very rich in faint stars
2438		in northern part of M46, needs high power or a nebular filter
2539		difficult in binoculars, excellent in a larger telescope, different stellar condensations, irregular circumference

STAR			Mag.	Spec.	Name, Comments	Dist.	R.A.	Dec.
5	γ	Mon	4.0	K3 III	. . . .	200 ly	6ʰ14.9	− 6°27
11	β	Mon	3.8	d B3 V	. . . .	800	6 28.8	− 7.03
14	ϑ	CMa	4.1	K4 III	. . . .	200	6 54.2	−12.04
18	μ	CMa	5.0	d G3 III	. . . .	500	6 56.1	−14.04
22	δ	Mon	4.2	A1 IV	. . . .	200	7 11.9	− 0.49
U		Mon	5.8–7.2	G4 Ib	. . . .	4000	7 30.8	− 9.78
26	α	Mon	3.9	K0 III	. . . .	200	7 41.2	− 9.55
2		Pup	5.7	d A3 V	. . . .	250	7 45.5	−14.69
5		Pup	5.5	d F5 IV	. . . .	200	7 47.9	−12.19
29	ζ	Mon	4.3	G2 Ib	. . . .	2000	8 08.6	− 2.98
19		Pup	4.7	d K0 III	. . . .	150	8 11.3	−12.93

BINARY			Mag.	Spec.	PA	Sep.	Vis.
11	β	Mon	4.5 5.4	B3 B3	132°	7.3	tl
			5.6	B3	106 C	2.8	tl
18	μ	CMa	5.1 7.9	G5!A2	340	3.0	tl
2		Pup	6.1 6.9	A2 A7	339	16.8	tl
5		Pup	5.6 7.6	F4 G3	0	1.8	Tl
19		Pup	4.7 7.8	K0 K	256	71	Bn

VARIABLE STAR

U Mon   semiregular
Period   92 d
pulsating star, similar to Mira type, light curve similar to β Lyrae type

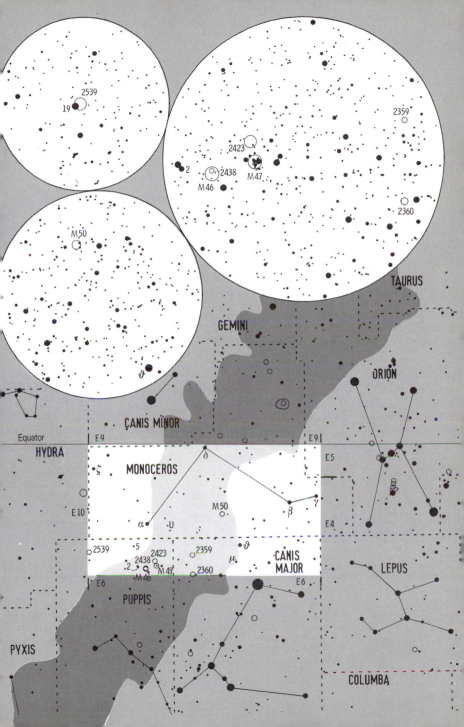

2539
19

2359

2423
2
2438
M46 M47

2360

M50

TAURUS

GEMINI

ORION

CANIS MINOR

Equator
E9   E9
HYDRA
                                      E5
ζ   MONOCEROS   δ
                                      E4
                               γ
                        M50
                          β
E10
        α   U
                                      E4
    2539   5
         2438 2423   2359   ϑ
      2   M47   2360   μ   CANIS
    M46   MAJOR   LEPUS
E6   E6
        PUPPIS

PYXIS

                                      COLUMBA

NEBULA	Const.	Mag.		Size	Shape	Type	Vis.	Dist.	R.A.	Dec.
2237	Mon	6^m	12$^m_{(5')}$	80$'$	Em2	Diff	bn	5 000 ly	6^{h}32^m	+ 5°0
2244	Mon	5	9	25	p n	Open	ey	5 000	6 32	+ 4.9
2301	Mon	6	8	15	m	Open	op	2 500	6 52	+ 0.5
2324	Mon	8½	9	8	r	Open	bn	15 000	7 04	+ 1.1
2632 M44	Cnc	3½	9	80	m	Open	ey	500	8 40	+20.0
2682 M67	Cnc	7	10	20	m	Open	op	2 500	8 51	+11.8

2237		**Rosette Nebula**, nebular filter recommended (NGC 2237–39, 2246)
2244		in Rosette Nebula, fine in binoculars, no better in a telescope
2301		partially resolved in binoculars, completely resolved in telescopes
2324		a large telescope shows an impressive number of stars
2632	M44	**Praesepe, Beehive**, easily visible with the unaided eye as a glow, impressive in binoculars, no better in a telescope
2682	M67	large nebula in binoculars, beautifully resolved in telescopes

STAR		Mag.	Spec.	Name, Comments	Dist.	R.A.	Dec.
8	ε Mon	4^{m}3	d A6 IV	not always designated	150 ly	6^{h}23^{m}8	+ 4°59
T	Mon	5.6–6.6	G4 Ib	. . . . . . ⌊ε Mon⌋	8 000	6 25.2	+ 7.09
3	β CMi	2.9	B8 V	Gomeisa	150	7 27.1	+ 8.29
4	γ CMi	4.3	K3 III	. . . .	200	7 28.2	+ 8.93
10	α CMi	0.4	F 5 IV	**Procyon**	11	7 39.3	+ 5.22
16	ζ Cnc	4.7	d G0 V	. . . .	70	8 12.2	+17.65
17	β Cnc	3.5	K4 III	Altarf	200	8 16.5	+ 9.19
23	φ^2 Cnc	5.6	d A4 IV	. . . .	400	8 26.8	+26.94
43	γ Cnc	4.7	A1 V	Asellus Borealis . .	150	8 43.3	+21.47
47	δ Cnc	3.9	K0 III	Asellus Australis . .	150	8 44.7	+18.15
48	ι Cnc	3.9	d G8 III	. . . .	300	8 46.7	+28.76
55	ϱ^1 Cnc	5.3	d K4 IV	companion is 53 Cnc	45	8 52.5	+28.30
57	Cnc	5.4	d G9 III	. . . .	600	8 54.2	+30.58
X	Cnc	5.6–7.5	C6 II	. . . .	2 000	8 55.4	+17.23
65	α Cnc	4.3	A5 V	Acubens	150	8 58.5	+11.86
RS	Cnc	5.0–5.6	M6 II	. . . .	2 000	9 10.6	+30.96

BINARY		Mag.		Spec.		PA	Sep.	Vis.
8	ε Mon	4^{m}4	6^{m}7	A5	F 5	27°	13″3	tl
16	ζ Cnc	5.6	6.0	F 8 G0	'90	182	0.6	-
					1995	125	0.7	-
					2000	86	0.8	Tl
					2005	59	1.0	Tl
					2010	38	1.1	Tl
			6.2		G4	72	6.0	tl
23	φ^2 Cnc	6.3	6.3	A3	A6	220	5.2	tl
48	ι Cnc	4.0	6.6	G6	A3	307	30.5	Bn
55	ϱ^1 Cnc	6.0	6.2	G8	M3	200	275	op
57	Cnc	6.0	6.4	G8	K0	310	1.4	Tl

VARIABLE STAR

T Mon		Cepheid
	Period	27.025 d
	Max.	2447919
	Min.	phase 0.73
	in 1960 period	
	was still 27.020 d	
X Cnc		semiregular
	Period	≈ 180 d
	reddish star	
RS Cnc		semiregular
	Period	≈ 120 d

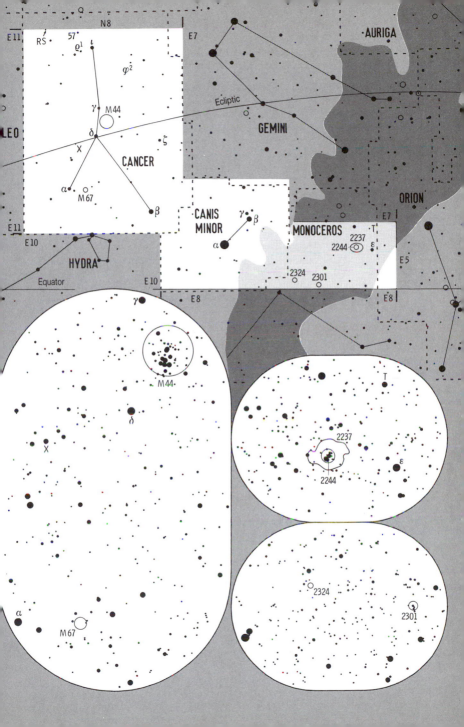

NEBULA		Const.	Mag.	Size	Shape	Type	Vis.	Dist.	R.A.	Dec.
2548	M48	Hya	$5\frac{1}{2}^m 10^m_{(5')}$	40'	m	Open	Ey	2500 ly	$8^h 14^m$	$- 5°8$
3115		Sex	$9\frac{1}{2}$ 9	5	L 7	Galx	bn	20 M	10 05	$- 7.7$
3242		Hya	9 4	0.6	D 1	Plan	Op	3 000	10 25	-18.6

2548	M48	fine bright open cluster in binoculars, not much better in a telescope, Messier's declination of M48 is 5° further north
3115		**Spindle Galaxy**, spindle shape only recognizable in telescopes at high power, fine edge-on galaxy with bright core
3242		**Ghost of Jupiter**, same size as Jupiter, high surface brightness, needs high power, greenish disk in a large telescope

STAR			Mag.	Spec.	Name, Comments	Dist.	R.A.	Dec.
C		Hya	3^m9	A0 V	. . . .	150 ly	$8^h 25^m7$	$- 3°91$
4	δ	Hya	4.2	A0 V	. . . .	150	8 37.7	$+ 5.70$
5	σ	Hya	4.4	K2 III	. . . .	150	8 38.8	$+ 3.34$
	β	Pyx	4.0	G5 II	. . . .	300	8 40.1	-35.31
7	η	Hya	4.3	B3 V	. . . .	500	8 43.2	$+ 3.40$
	α	Pyx	3.7	B2 III	. . . .	1 200	8 43.6	-33.19
11	ε	Hya	3.4	d G0 III	. . . .	150	8 46.8	$+ 6.42$
13	ϱ	Hya	4.4	A0 V	. . . .	150	8 48.4	$+ 5.84$
	γ	Pyx	4.0	K4 III	. . . .	200	8 50.5	-27.71
16	ζ	Hya	3.1	K0 III	. . . .	150	8 55.4	$+ 5.95$
22	ϑ	Hya	3.9	A0 V	. . . .	150	9 14.4	$+ 2.31$
27		Hya	4.7	d G6 III	. . . .	150	9 20.5	$- 9.56$
30	α	Hya	2.0	K3 III	**Alphard**	90	9 27.6	$- 8.66$
31	$τ^1$	Hya	4.5	d F 7 V	. . . .	50	9 29.1	$- 2.77$
35	ι	Hya	3.9	K3 III	. . . .	200	9 39.9	$- 1.14$
39	$υ^1$	Hya	4.1	G8 III	. . . .	150	9 51.5	-14.85
8	γ	Sex	5.1	d A2 V	. . . .	300	9 52.5	$- 8.11$
15	α	Sex	4.5	B9 IV	. . . .	300	10 07.9	$- 0.37$
41	λ	Hya	3.6	K0 III	. . . .	150	10 10.6	-12.35
42	μ	Hya	3.8	K4 III	. . . .	200	10 26.1	-16.84
	α	Ant	4.3	K6 III	. . . .	200	10 27.2	-31.07
U		Hya	4.7–5.2	C6 II	. . . .	2 000	10 37.6	-13.38
35		Sex	5.8	d K2 III	. . . .	800	10 43.3	$+ 4.75$
	ν	Hya	3.1	K2 III	. . . .	120	10 49.6	-16.19

BINARY			Mag.	Spec.	PA	Sep.	Vis.
11	ε	Hya	3^m4 7^m0	G0 F 7 '90	294°	2"7	Tl
				2010	310	2.7	Tl
27		Hya	4.8 7.0	G8 F 2	211	230	Op
31	$τ^1$	Hya	4.6 7.6	F6 K2	3	66	Bn
8	γ	Sex	5.6 6.1	A1 A4 '90	67	0.6	-
				2010	45	0.6	-
35		Sex	6.1 7.2	K3 K0	240	6.8	tl

VARIABLE STAR

U Hya semiregular
Period ≈ 450 d
especially red
during minimum
light, exhibits a
large amplitude
in blue light

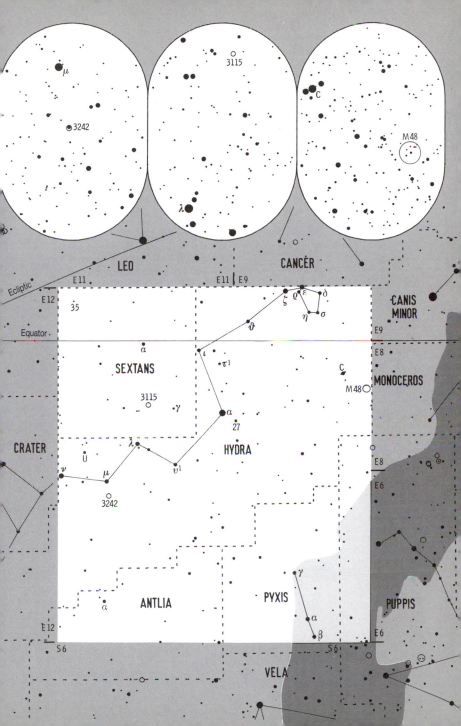

NEBULA		Const.	Mag.		Size	Shape	Type	Vis.	Dist.	R.A.	Dec.
2903		Leo	9^m	9$^m_{(5')}$	8$'$	Sb 6	Galx	bn	20 M ly	9^{h}32^m	+21°5
3351	M95	Leo	10	9	4	Sb 3	Galx	Bn	30 M	10 44	+11.7
3368	M96	Leo	9½	9	5	Sb 3	Galx	bn	30 M	10 47	+11.8
3379	M105	Leo	9½	8	3	E 1	Galx	bn	30 M	10 48	+12.6
3384		Leo	10	8	4	L 7	Galx	Bn	30 M	10 48½	+12.6
3623	M65	Leo	9½	9	8	Sa 8	Galx	bn	30 M	11 19	+13.1
3627	M66	Leo	9	9	8	Sb 6	Galx	bn	30 M	11 20	+13.0
3628		Leo	10	9	12	Sb 9	Galx	Bn	30 M	11 20	+13.6

2903		galaxy with bright oval center, relatively easy to find
3351	M95	stellar core, arms of barred spiral too faint for amateur telescopes
3368	M96	quite elongated central area, stellar core
3379	M105	rather more easily visible than M95 and M96, stellar core
3384		only 8$'$ east of M105, stellar core within featureless nebula
3623	M65	circular central region, but very elongated nebulous halo
3627	M66	visible in binoculars, becomes interesting only in large telescopes, irregular shape, dark dust features barely observable
3628		nicely elongated, faint dust lane along the southern edge

STAR			Mag.	Spec.	Name, Comments	Dist.	R.A.	Dec.
2	ω	Leo	5^{m}4	d F 9 V	. . . .	120 ly	9^{h}28^{m}5	+ 9°06
4	λ	Leo	4.3	K5 III	Alterf	250	9 31.7	+22.97
14	o	Leo	3.5	A5 V	. . . .	70	9 41.1	+ 9.89
17	ε	Leo	3.0	G0 II	. . . .	300	9 45.9	+23.77
R		Leo	4.4–11.3	M7 III	. . . .	300	9 47.6	+11.43
24	μ	Leo	3.9	K2 III	. . . .	200	9 52.8	+26.01
30	η	Leo	3.5	A0 Ib	. . . .	2 000	10 07.3	+16.76
32	α	Leo	1.4	B7 V	**Regulus**	80	10 08.4	+11.97
36	ζ	Leo	3.4	F0 III	Aldhafera	120	10 16.7	+23.42
41	γ	Leo	2.1	d K0 III	Algieba	150	10 20.0	+19.84
47	ϱ	Leo	3.9	B1 Ib	. . . .	2 500	10 32.8	+ 9.31
54		Leo	4.3	d A1 V	. . . .	200	10 55.6	+24.75
68	δ	Leo	2.6	A4 V	Zosma	60	11 14.1	+20.52
70	ϑ	Leo	3.3	A2 V	Coxa	80	11 14.2	+15.43
78	ι	Leo	3.9	d F 3 IV	. . . .	70	11 23.9	+10.53
94	β	Leo	2.1	A3 V	**Denebola**	40	11 49.1	+14.57

BINARY			Mag.	Spec.		PA	Sep.	Vis.
2	ω	Leo	5^{m}9 6^{m}5	F 9	G ’90	53°	0$''$5	-
					2000	84	0.6	-
					2010	103	0.7	-
41	γ	Leo	2.4 3.6	K1	G7	125	4.4	tl
54		Leo	4.5 6.3	A1	A2	112	6.6	tl
78	ι	Leo	4.0 6.7	F 2	G3 ’90	131	1.5	Tl
					2010	105	2.0	Tl

VARIABLE STAR

R Leo	Mira type
Period	≈ 311 d
Max.	≈ 2448200
Min.	phase 0.57
Mean	5^{m}8–10^{m}0
period varies	
by a few days	

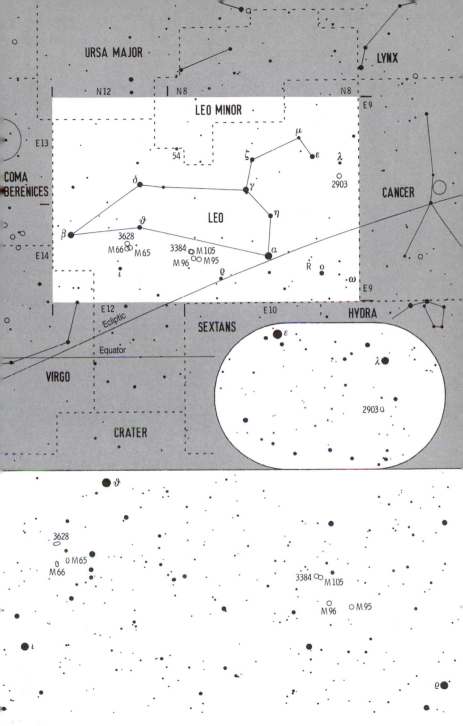

NEBULA	Const.	Mag.		Size	Shape	Type	Vis.	Dist.	R.A.	Dec.
4361		Crv	11^m $8^m_{(5')}$	$1'.5$	D 0	Plan	Bn	4 000 ly	12^h24^m	$-18°.8$
4590	M68	Hya	8 10	8	X	Glob	Op	30 000	12 39½	−26.7
4594	M104	Vir	8½ 8	8	Sa 7	Galx	Op	40 M	12 40	−11.6
4697		Vir	9½ 8	3	E 5	Galx	bn	50 M	12 48½	− 5.8

4361	faint planetary, requires high magnification, faint 13^m central star
4590 M68	resolved only in large telescopes, but then even in the very center
4594 M104	**Sombrero Galaxy**, very elongated, spindle shape barely visible
	in binoculars, impressive in a large telescope, dust lane
	nearly right through the center, stellar core
4697	small and elongated, featureless nebula in a telescope

STAR			Mag.	Spec.	Name, Comments	Dist.	R.A.	Dec.
7	α	Crt	$4^m.1$	K0 III	Alkes	120 ly	$10^h59^m.8$	$-18°.30$
11	β	Crt	4.5	A 2 III	. . . .	200	11 11.7	−22.83
12	δ	Crt	3.6	G8 III	. . . .	90	11 19.3	−14.78
15	γ	Crt	4.1	A 5 V	. . . .	100	11 24.9	−17.68
84	τ	Leo	4.9	d G8 III	. . . .	400	11 27.9	+ 2.85
N		Hya	5.0	d F 8 V	. . . .	100	11 32.3	−29.26
	ξ	Hya	3.5	G7 III	. . . .	150	11 33.0	−31.86
3	ν	Vir	4.0	M1 III	. . . .	150	11 45.9	+ 6.53
5	β	Vir	3.6	F 8 V	Zavijava	32	11 50.7	+ 1.76
	β	Hya	4.3	B 9 III	. . . .	300	11 52.9	−33.91
1	α	Crv	4.0	F 2 IV	Alchiba	70	12 08.4	−24.73
2	ε	Crv	3.0	K2 III	. . . .	100	12 10.1	−22.62
4	γ	Crv	2.6	B 8 III	Gienah	200	12 15.8	−17.54
15	η	Vir	3.9	A 2 IV	Zaniah	150	12 19.9	− 0.67
7	δ	Crv	3.0	B 9 V	Algorab	120	12 29.9	−16.52
9	β	Crv	2.7	G5 II	. . . .	300	12 34.4	−23.40
26	χ	Vir	4.7	K2 III	. . . .	250	12 39.2	− 8.00
29	γ	Vir	2.8	d F 0 V	Porrima	35	12 41.7	− 1.45
46	γ	Hya	3.0	G6 III	. . . .	100	13 18.9	−23.17
R		Hya	3.5–10.9	M7 III	. . . .	500	13 29.7	−23.28

BINARY			Mag.	Spec.	PA	Sep.	Vis.
84	τ	Leo	$5^m.0$ $7^m.6$	G8 G4	$180°$	$88''$	bn
N		Hya	5.6 5.8	F 8 F 8	210	9.2	tl
29	γ	Vir	3.5 3.5	F 0 F 0 '90	287	3.0	tl
					1995 280	2.5	tl
					2000 267	1.8	tl
		minimum separation			2002 259	1.5	tl
		$0''.4$ in December 2007,			2004 246	1.2	Tl
		rotation $6°$ per month			2006 221	0.8	Tl
					2008 126	0.4	-
					2010 44	0.9	Tl

VARIABLE STAR

R Hya	Mira type
Period	389 d
Max.	2447910
Min.	phase 0.52
Mean	$4^m.5$–$9^m.5$

period has been
decreasing, it was
about 500 days at
the beginning of
the 18th century

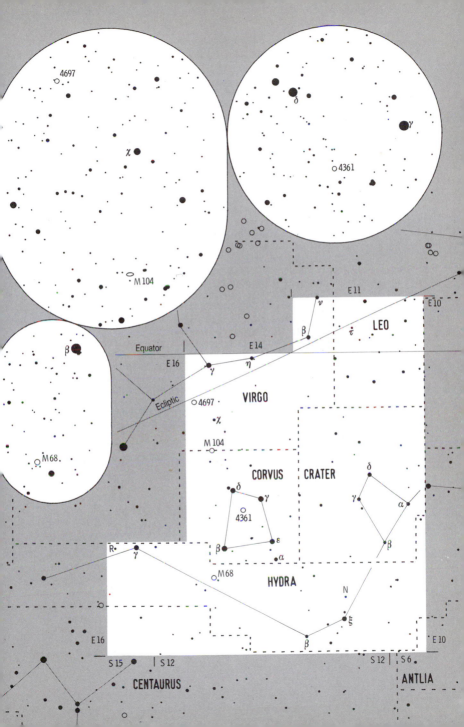

NEBULA	Const.	Mag.		Size	Shape	Type	Vis.	Dist.	R.A.	Dec.
Coma Cluster	Com	$2\frac{1}{2}^m$	$11^m_{(5')}$	300'	p	Open	ey	250 ly	12^h25^m	$+26°0$
4494	Com	10	9	3	E 2	Galx	Bn	40 M	12 31½	+25.8
4559	Com	10	10	8	Sc 6	Galx	Bn	40 M	12 36	+28.0
4565	Com	10	10	15	Sb 9	Galx	Bn	40 M	12 36	+26.0
4631	CVn	9½	9	12	Sd 9	Galx	bn	30 M	12 42	+32.5
4656	CVn	10½	10	15	Sm9	Galx	tl	30 M	12 44	+32.2
4725	Com	9½	11	10	Sb 4	Galx	Bn	40 M	12 50	+25.5
4826 M64	Com	8½	8	6	Sb 5	Galx	Op	30 M	12 57	+21.7
5024 M53	Com	8	9	8	V	Glob	Op	60 000	13 13	+18.2

Coma Cluster	distinctly visible with unaided eye under dark sky when some individual stars are visible, fine in opera glasses, almost too big for binoculars, completely inconspicuous in a telescope
4494	quite bright core, very irregular nebulosity
4559	distinctly elongated, features hardly visible in amateur telescopes
4565	wonderful edge-on galaxy, nearly central dust lane, very long, faint object, therefore large aperture is needed
4631	edge-on like NGC 4565, but no dust lane, many irregular knots and asymmetries visible in large telescopes
4656	difficult edge-on galaxy, modest bright central region, the other condensation 3' northeast of the core is NGC 4657
4725	the small core is visible in large telescopes, but not the bar, outer portion needs lowest magnification and darkest sky
4826 M64	**Black Eye Galaxy**, elongated absorption next to the core just visible in large telescopes, outer edge of the galaxy is sharp and not diffuse like most galaxies
5024 M53	distinct core, outer region partially resolved in a telescope

STAR		Mag.	Spec.	Name, Comments	Dist.	R.A.	Dec.
2	Com	5.7	d F0 IV	. . . .	250 ly	$12^h04.3$	$+21°46$
15 γ	Com	4.4	K1 III	in Coma Cluster . .	250	12 26.9	+28.27
17	Com	5.0	d A0 V	in Coma Cluster . .	250	12 28.9	+25.91
24	Com	4.8	d G8 III	. . . .	250	12 35.1	+18.38
32	Com	5.8	d K0 III	. . . .	250	12 52.3	+17.09
35	Com	4.9	d G7 III	. . . .	250	12 53.3	+21.24
42 α	Com	4.3	F 5 V	Diadem	60	13 10.0	+17.53
43 β	Com	4.3	G0 V	. . . .	27	13 11.9	+27.88

BINARY		Mag.	Spec.	PA	Sep.	Vis.
2	Com	5.9 7.4	F0 A9	237°	3.7	tl
17	Com	5.3 6.6	A0 A1	251	145	Op
24	Com	5.0 6.6	K2!A9	271	20.3	tl
32	Com	6.3 6.9	K7 F8	49	196	Op
35	Com	5.1 7.2	G8 F 5 '90	173	1.1	Tl
			2010	190	1.2	Tl

Comm.: Coma Cluster

1) The group of stars visible by unaided eye.

2) Sometimes the Coma Galaxy Cluster 250 M ly distant is called the Coma Cluster.

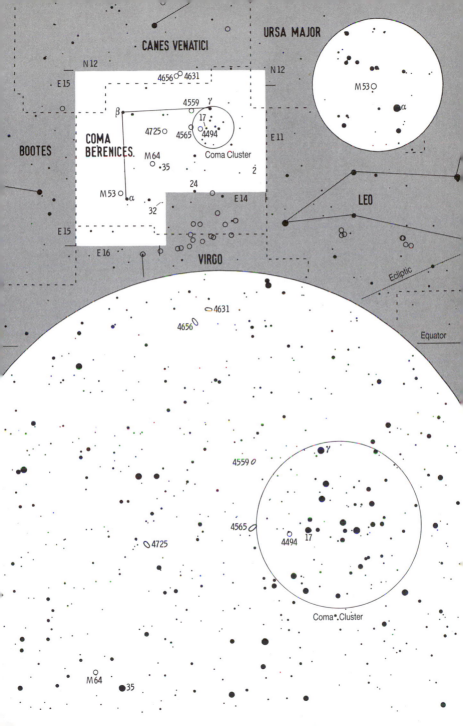

CANES VENATICI

URSA MAJOR

N 12

N 12

E 15

4656 ○ ○ 4631

M 53 ○

4559 γ

β

17

○ α

4725 ○

4565

4494

E 11

COMA
BERENICES.

Coma Cluster

M 64

2

BOOTES

35

E 15

M 53 ○

α

24

E 14

LEO

32

E 15

E 16

φ

VIRGO

Ecliptic

4631

Equator

4656

4559 ○

4565 ○

4494 ○ 17

4725 ○

γ

Coma Cluster

M 64

35

NEBULA		Const.	Mag.		Size	Shape		Type	Vis.	Dist.	R.A.	Dec.
4192	M98	Com	10^m	$10^m_{(5')}$	8'	Sb	7	Galx	Bn	50 M ly	12^h14^m	$+14°9$
4216		Vir	10	9	8	Sb	9	Galx	Bn	50 M	12 16	+13.1
4254	M99	Com	10	10	4	Sc	1	Galx	Bn	50 M	12 19	+14.4
4303	M61	Vir	10	10	5	Sb	1	Galx	Bn	50 M	12 22	+ 4.5
4321	M100	Com	9½	9	5	Sb	2	Galx	bn	50 M	12 23	+15.8
4374	M84	Vir	9½	8	3	E	1	Galx	Bn	50 M	12 25	+12.9
4382	M85	Com	9½	9	4	L	3	Galx	Bn	50 M	12 25½	+18.2
4406	M86	Vir	9½	9	4	E	3	Galx	Bn	50 M	12 26	+12.9
	3C 273	Vir	13	(4)	< 0.1	stellar		Quasar	Tl	2 000 M	12 29.1	+2.05
4472	M49	Vir	8½	8	5	E	2	Galx	bn	40 M	12 30	+ 8.0
4486	M87	Vir	9	8	4	E	1	Galx	bn	50 M	12 31	+12.4
4501	M88	Com	9½	9	6	Sb	5	Galx	Bn	50 M	12 32	+14.4
4526		Vir	10	9	5	L	7	Galx	Bn	40 M	12 34	+ 7.7
4548	M91	Com	10½	10	4	Sb	2	Galx	tl	50 M	12 35½	+14.5
4552	M89	Vir	10	9	2.5	E	0	Galx	Bn	50 M	12 35½	+12.5
4569	M90	Vir	10	10	8	Sb	7	Galx	Bn	50 M	12 37	+13.2
4579	M58	Vir	10	10	5	Sb	2	Galx	Bn	50 M	12 38	+11.8
4621	M59	Vir	10	9	3	E	4	Galx	Bn	50 M	12 42	+11.6
4649	M60	Vir	9	8	4	E	2	Galx	bn	50 M	12 43½	+11.6
4762		Vir	10½	8	5	L	9	Galx	Bn	50 M	12 53	+11.2

The **Virgo Cluster** is the nearest of the rich clusters of galaxies. The central region is marked on the chart. The whole area of the cluster includes galaxies in charts N10–N14 and E10–E14. In the center, faint galaxies are so abundant that it is hard to find one's way around.

4192	M98	distinctly elongated galaxy with faint diffuse halo
4216		fine, remarkable edge-on galaxy, though very faint
4254	M99	bright central area, larger telescopes indicate light patches and a hint of the spiral arms, but no nucleus
4303	M61	spiral arms are only just visible in large telescopes
4321	M100	elongated central area with a stellar nucleus, no other features
4374	M84	bright featureless glow, within a region of many 12^m galaxies
4382	M85	diffuse oval, bright elongated core, 8' east is 11^m galaxy NGC 4394
4406	M86	featureless, **Makarian's Galaxy Chain** up to M88, galaxies 10^m–11^m
	3C 273	brightest **Quasar**, probably active, especially bright nucleus of a galaxy at enormous distance, very faint stellar dot
4472	M49	brightest galaxy of the Virgo Cluster, large elliptical galaxy
4486	M87	**Virgo A**, central galaxy of the Virgo Cluster, bright core
4501	M88	faint detail in large telescopes, **Makarian's Galaxy Chain** to M86
4526		asymmetric, nucleus not centered in the galaxy, takes high power
4548	M91	featureless, Messier's M91 not uniquely identified as NGC 4548
4552	M89	round glow with a bright, nearly stellar core
4569	M90	bright central elongated area, largest galaxy of the Virgo Cluster
4579	M58	the bar of the barred spiral can be seen in a large telescope
4621	M59	stellar core, but not very distinct, best at medium power
4649	M60	intense stellar core, 4' northwest is 12^m galaxy NGC 4647
4762		faint spindle, elongated core, 10' northwest is 11^m galaxy NGC 4754

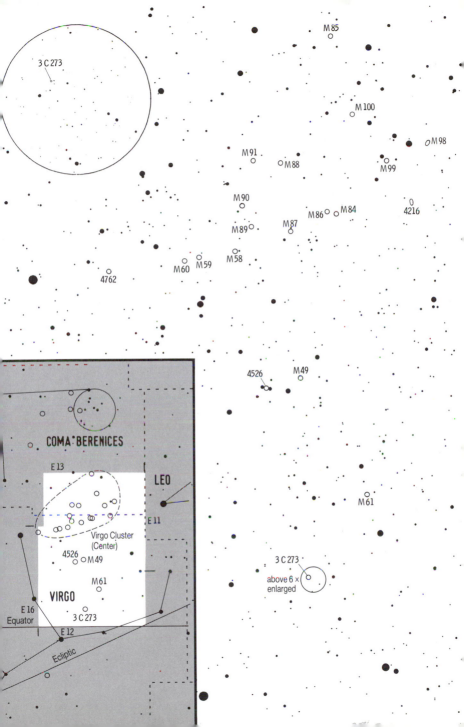

NEBULA		Const.	Mag.		Size	Shape	Type	Vis.	Dist.	R.A.		Dec.
5272	M3	CVn	$6\frac{1}{2}^m$	$8^m_{(5')}$	10$'$	VI	Glob	Ey	30 000 ly	13^{h}42^m		+28°.4
5746		Vir	11	9	6	Sb 9	Galx	tl	60 M	14 45		+ 1.9
5904	M5	Ser	6	8	12	V	Glob	Ey	25 000	15 18½		+ 2.1

5272	M3	bright, easy to see, but hard to find, resolved in large telescopes
5746		very faint edge-on galaxy for large telescopes
5904	M5	excellent, especially in a large telescope, slightly elliptical, relatively easily resolved, several dense areas

STAR			Mag.	Spec.	Name, Comments	Dist.	R.A.	Dec.
5	υ	Boo	4.1	K5 III	. . . .	250 ly	13^{h}49^m.5	+15°.80
8	η	Boo	2.7	G0 IV	Muphrid	30	13 54.7	+18.40
16	α	Boo	0.0	K2 III	**Arcturus**	35	14 15.7	+19.18
25	ϱ	Boo	3.6	K3 III	. . . .	200	14 31.8	+30.37
29	π	Boo	4.6	d A1 V	. . . .	200	14 40.7	+16.42
30	ζ	Boo	3.8	d A2 III	. . . .	300	14 41.1	+13.73
34		Boo	4.7–5.4	M3 III	W Bootis	400	14 43.4	+26.53
36	ε	Boo	2.4	d G9 III	Izar, Pulcherrima . .	150	14 45.0	+27.07
109		Vir	3.7	A0 V	. . . .	120	14 46.2	+ 1.89
37	ξ	Boo	4.6	d G8 V	. . . .	22	14 51.4	+19.10
2	η	CrB	5.0	d G2 V	. . . .	55	15 23.2	+30.29
3	β	CrB	3.7	A9 III	Nusakan	120	15 27.8	+29.11
4	ϑ	CrB	4.1	B6 V	. . . .	300	15 32.9	+31.36
5	α	CrB	2.3	A0 V	**Alphekka, Gemma** .	80	15 34.7	+26.71
8	γ	CrB	3.8	d A0 IV	. . . .	200	15 42.7	+26.30
R		CrB	5.7–14.8	G0 II	. . . .	4000	15 48.6	+28.16
10	δ	CrB	4.6	G4 III	. . . .	150	15 49.6	+26.07
13	ε	CrB	4.2	K2 III	. . . .	250	15 57.6	+26.88

BINARY			Mag.	Spec.	PA	Sep.	Vis.
29	π	Boo	4.9 5.8	B9 A6	111°	5".5	tl
30	ζ	Boo	4.5 4.6	A2 A2 '90	303	1.0	Tl
				2000	300	0.8	Tl
				2010	295	0.6	-
36	ε	Boo	2.5 4.9	K0! A2	340	2.8	tl
37	ξ	Boo	4.7 7.0	G8 K4 '90	326	7.0	tl
				2010	308	6.0	tl
2	η	CrB	5.6 5.9	G1 G3 '90	27	1.0	Tl
				1995	43	0.9	Tl
				2000	65	0.7	-
				2005	110	0.5	-
				2010	169	0.6	-
8	γ	CrB	4.1 5.5	A0 A3 '90	118	0.6	-
				2000	114	0.8	Tl
				2010	110	0.6	-

VARIABLE STAR

34 W Boo semiregular
Period   30–450 d
R CrB   irregular
A subgroup of
irregular variable
stars is named
after R CrB:
giants, usually
staying near
maximum light,
rapid decrease
in brightness,
followed by an
increase lasting
several months.

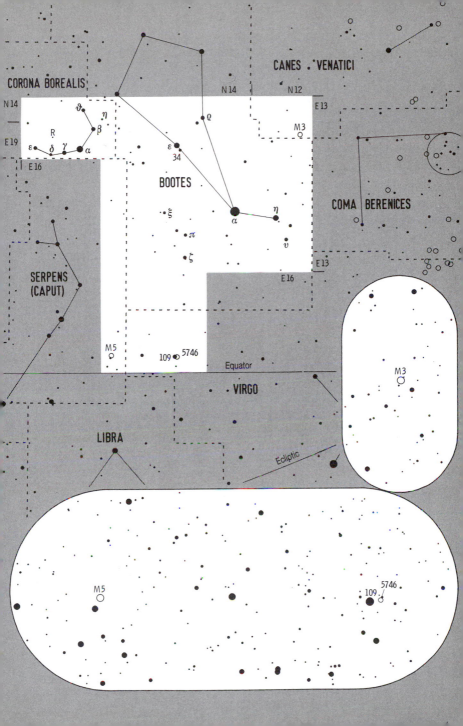

NEBULA	Const.	Mag.		Size	Shape	Type	Vis.	Dist.	R.A.	Dec.
5236 M83	Hya	8^m	9$^m_{(5')}$	10$'$	Sc 1	Galx	Op	15 Mly	13^{h}37^m	−29.°9

5236 M83	easy object for binoculars, beautiful in a large telescope, bright condensed core, elongated bar, traces of spiral arms

STAR			Mag.	Spec.	Name, Comments	Dist.	R.A.	Dec.
43	δ	Vir	3^{m}4	M3 III	. . . .	150 ly	12^{h}55^{m}6	+ 3.°40
47	ϵ	Vir	2.8	G9 III	Vindemiatrix . . .	100	13 02.2	+10.96
51	ϑ	Vir	4.4	A1 V	. . . .	150	13 09.9	− 5.54
67	α	Vir	1.0	B1 IV	**Spica**	300	13 25.2	−11.16
79	ζ	Vir	3.4	A3 V	. . . .	80	13 34.7	− 0.60
3		Cen	4.3	dB5 IV	. . . .	500	13 51.8	−32.99
93	τ	Vir	4.3	A3 V	. . . .	100	14 01.6	+ 1.54
49	π	Hya	3.3	K2 III	. . . .	100	14 06.4	−26.68
107	μ	Vir	3.9	F3 IV	. . . .	100	14 43.1	− 5.66
54		Hya	4.9	dF3 IV	. . . .	100	14 46.0	−25.44
7	μ	Lib	5.3	dA2 V	. . . .	250	14 49.3	−14.15
9,8	α	Lib	2.6	dA4 IV	Zubenelgenubi . . .	70	14 50.9	−16.04
19	δ	Lib	4.9–5.9	A0 V	. . . .	250	15 01.0	− 8.52
20	σ	Lib	3.3	M4 III	. . . .	120	15 04.1	−25.28
27	β	Lib	2.6	B8 V	Zubeneschemali . .	120	15 17.0	− 9.38
13	δ	Ser	3.8	dF0 IV	. . . .	120	15 34.8	+10.54
38	γ	Lib	3.9	G8 IV	. . . .	80	15 35.5	−14.79
39	υ	Lib	3.6	K4 III	. . . .	120	15 37.0	−28.13
40	τ	Lib	3.7	B3 V	. . . .	400	15 38.7	−29.78
24	α	Ser	2.7	K2 III	Unukalhai	80	15 44.3	+ 6.43
28	β	Ser	3.7	A2 IV	. . . .	120	15 46.2	+15.42
35	κ	Ser	4.1	M1 III	. . . .	250	15 48.7	+18.14
32	μ	Ser	3.5	A0 V	. . . .	150	15 49.6	− 3.43
R		Ser	5.2–14.4	M6 III	. . . .	800	15 50.7	+15.13
37	ϵ	Ser	3.7	A2 V	. . . .	100	15 50.8	+ 4.48
5	χ	Lup	4.0	B9 IV	. . . .	200	15 51.0	−33.63
41	γ	Ser	3.9	F6 V	. . . .	40	15 56.5	+15.66
	ξ	Lup	4.6	dA1 V	. . . .	250	15 56.9	−33.97
	ξ	Sco	4.1	dF6 IV	. . . .	80	16 04.4	−11.37

BINARY			Mag.		Spec.		PA	Sep.	Vis.
3		Cen	4^{m}6	6^{m}1	B5	B8	107°	7$''$8	tl
54		Hya	5.1	7.0	F1	G2	122	8.3	tl
7	μ	Lib	5.7	6.6	A1	A5	4	2.0	tl
9,8	α	Lib	2.8	5.2	A3	F4	314	231	op
13	δ	Ser	4.2	5.2	F0	F0 '90	177	4.3	tl
						2010	175	4.5	tl
	ξ	Lup	5.2	5.6	A0	A2	49	10.4	tl
	ξ	Sco	4.2	7.3	F5	G7	47	7.7	tl

VARIABLE STAR

19 δ Lib	Algol type
Period	2.32736 d
Min.	2447894.71
Max. ph.0.11–0.89	
R Ser	Mira type
Period	356.4 d
Max.	2448016
Min.	phase 0.59

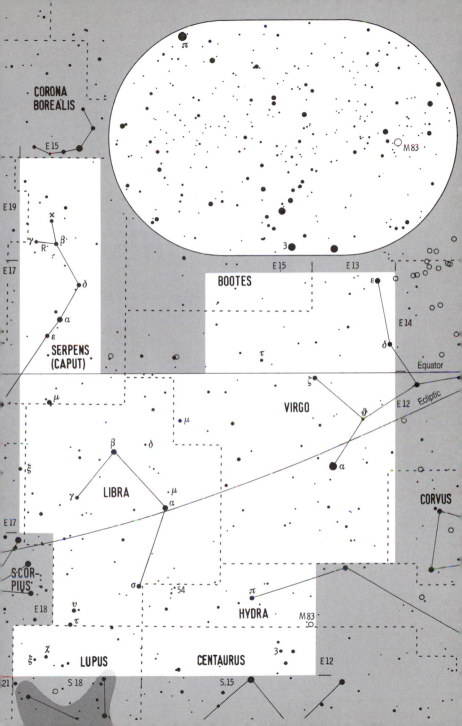

NEBULA		Const.	Mag.		Size	Shape	Type	Vis.	Dist.	R.A.	Dec.
6171	M107	Oph	8^m	9$^m_{(5')}$	6$'$	X	Glob	Op	20000ly	16^{h}32$\frac{1}{2}^m$	−13°1
6218	M12	Oph	6$\frac{1}{2}$	9	12	IX	Glob	op	20000	16 47	− 2.0
6254	M10	Oph	6$\frac{1}{2}$	9	12	VII	Glob	op	15000	16 57	− 4.1
6333	M9	Oph	8	9	6	VIII	Glob	Op	25000	17 19	−18.5
6402	M14	Oph	7$\frac{1}{2}$	9	8	VIII	Glob	Op	40000	17 37$\frac{1}{2}$	− 3.2
IC 4665		Oph	5	10	50	p	Open	Ey	1200	17 46	+ 5.7

6171 M107   very difficult to resolve even in a large telescope
6218 M12   slightly elliptical glow in binoculars, well resolved in a telescope, looks almost like some of the rich open clusters
6254 M10   center partially resolved, outer region well resolved in large scopes
6333 M9   barely resolvable, similar globular cluster (NGC 6356) 1° northeast
6402 M14   oval nebula, individual stars too faint for amateur telescopes
IC 4665   conspicuous in opera glasses and binoculars, but not in telescopes

STAR			Mag.	Spec.	Name, Comments	Dist.	R.A.	Dec.
1	δ	Oph	2^{m}7	M1 III	Yed Prior	150ly	16^{h}14^{m}3	− 3°69
2	ε	Oph	3.2	G9 III	Yed Posterior . . .	100	16 18.3	− 4.69
7	χ	Oph	4.2–5.0	B2 V	. . . .	600	16 27.0	−18.46
10	λ	Oph	3.8	d A2 V	Marfik	150	16 30.9	+ 1.98
13	ζ	Oph	2.6	O9 V	. . . .	600	16 37.2	−10.57
27	κ	Oph	3.2	K2 III	. . . .	120	16 57.7	+ 9.38
35	η	Oph	2.4	A2 V	Sabik	60	17 10.4	−15.72
55	α	Oph	2.1	A5 III	Rasalhague	60	17 34.9	+12.56
55	ξ	Ser	3.5	F0 IV	. . . .	80	17 37.6	−15.40
60	β	Oph	2.8	K2 III	Cebalrai	120	17 43.5	+ 4.57
61		Oph	5.6	d A0 V	. . . .	500	17 44.6	+ 2.58
62	γ	Oph	3.8	A0 V	. . . .	100	17 47.9	+ 2.71
Barnard			9.5	M5 V	Barnard's Star . . .	6.0	17 57.8	+ 4.69
64	ν	Oph	3.3	K0 III	. . . .	150	17 59.0	− 9.77
67		Oph	4.0	B5 Ib	. . . . : . .	2500	18 00.6	+ 2.93
69	τ	Oph	4.8	d F3 V	. . . .	100	18 03.1	− 8.18
70		Oph	4.0	d K1 V	. . . .	17	18 05.5	+ 2.50
72		Oph	3.7	A4 V	. . . .	80	18 07.3	+ 9.56

BINARY			Mag.		Spec.		PA	Sep.	Vis.
10	λ	Oph	4^{m}2	5^{m}2	A1	A4	30°	1$''$5	tl
61		Oph	6.2	6.6	A0	A0	93	20.6	Bn
69	τ	Oph	5.2	5.9	F3	F4 '90	280	1.8	tl
						2010	288	1.6	tl
70		Oph	4.2	6.0	K0	K4 '90	224	1.5	Tl
						1995	168	2.5	tl
						2000	148	3.8	tl
						2005	138	4.9	tl
						2010	131	5.7	tl

VARIABLE STAR

7 χ Oph   irregular

Note: Barnard's Star
Fastest star, largest
proper motion of
10$''$ per year, also nearest star in northern
hemisphere, α Cen =
Toliman is closer still

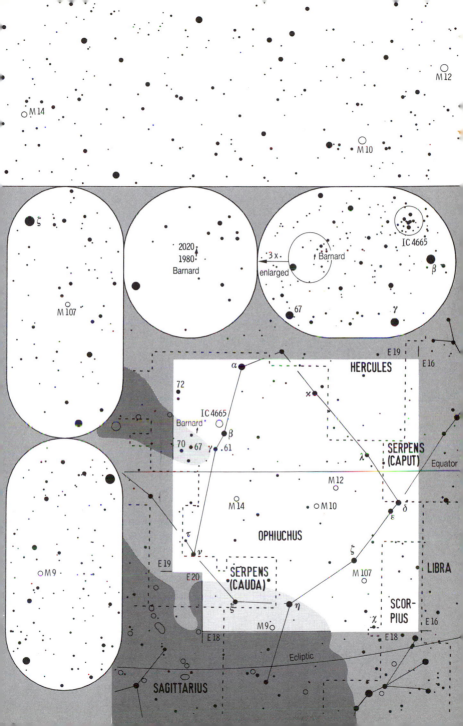

NEBULA	Const.	Mag.		Size	Shape	Type	Vis.	Dist.	R.A.	Dec.
6093 M80	Sco	$7\frac{1}{2}^m$	$7\frac{m}{(5')}$	$5'$	II	Glob	op	30000 ly	16^h17^m	$-23°.0$
6121 M4	Sco	6	9	20	IX	Glob	op	8000	16 24	-26.5
6266 M62	Oph	$6\frac{1}{2}$	8	10	IV	Glob	op	20000	17 01	-30.1
6273 M19	Oph	7	8	8	VIII	Glob	op	30000	$17\ 02\frac{1}{2}$	-26.3
6369	Oph	11	6	0.5	R 0	Plan	Bn	6000	$17\ 29\frac{1}{2}$	-23.8
6405 M6	Sco	$4\frac{1}{2}$	7	20	m	Open	ey	2000	17 40	-32.2
6475 M7	Sco	$3\frac{1}{2}$	8	50	m	Open	ey	1000	17 54	-34.8

6093	M80	very bright central area, takes high magnification
6121	M4	easy to find, easy to see, beautifully resolved in telescopes
6266	M62	slightly asymmetric, nebulous arms, interesting globular cluster
6273	M19	quite oval, edges can be resolved into stars
6369		stellar at low power, disk at high power, but hardly a ring
6405	M6	**Butterfly Cluster**, excellent object for every scope
6475	M7	easily visible by unaided eye, nicely resolved in opera glasses, not better in a telescope, southernmost Messier object

STAR		Mag.	Spec.	Name, Comments	Dist.	R.A.	Dec.
5	ϱ Sco	$3^m.9$	B 2 V	. . . .	600 ly	$15^h56^m.9$	$-29°.21$
6	π Sco	2.9	B 1 V	. . . .	600	15 58.9	-26.11
7	δ Sco	2.3	B 0 IV	. . . .	800	16 00.3	-22.62
8	β Sco	2.5	d B 1 IV	Acrab	800	16 05.4	-19.80
9	ω^1 Sco	4.0	B 1 V	. . . .	800	16 06.8	-20.67
14	ν Sco	3.9	d B 3 V	. . . .	600	16 12.0	-19.46
20	σ Sco	2.9	B 1 III	. . . .	600	16 21.2	-25.59
5	ϱ Oph	4.4	d B 2 IV	. . . .	1200	16 25.6	-23.44
21	α Sco	0.9–1.8 d M0 Ib		**Antares**	500	16 29.4	-26.43
23	τ Sco	2.8	B 0 V	. . . .	800	16 35.9	-28.22
26	ε Sco	2.3	K 2 III	. . . .	70	16 50.2	-34.29
RR	Sco	5.0–12.4 M6 III		. . . .	1000	16 56.6	-30.58
36	Oph	4.3	d K0 V	. . . .	18	17 15.3	-26.60
39	o Oph	5.0	d G8 III	. . . .	300	17 18.0	-24.29
42	ϑ Oph	3.3	B 2 IV	. . . .	600	17 22.0	-25.00

BINARY		Mag.		Spec.		PA	Sep.	Vis.
8	β Sco	$2^m.6$	$4^m.9$	B 1	B 2	$21°$	$13''.6$	tl
14	ν Sco	4.0	6.7	B 2	B 9	337	41.1	Bn
			7.8		B 9	55 C	2.7	tl
5	ϱ Oph	5.0	5.7	B 2	B 2	337	2.8	tl
			6.7		B 3	253	156	Op
			7.2		B 7	1	151	Op
21	α Sco	1–2	5.5	M1!	B 3	273	2.6	Tl
36	Oph	5.1	5.1	K0	K1 '90	151	4.8	tl
					2010	143	5.1	tl
39	o Oph	5.2	6.8	K1	F 6	355	10.3	tl

VARIABLE STAR

21 α Sco semiregular
   Period   4–5 years
   Mean $0^m.9$–$1^m.1$
   difficult binary
   with highly con-
   trasting colors

RR Sco   Mira type
   Period   280 d
   Max.   2447948
   Min. Phase 0.53

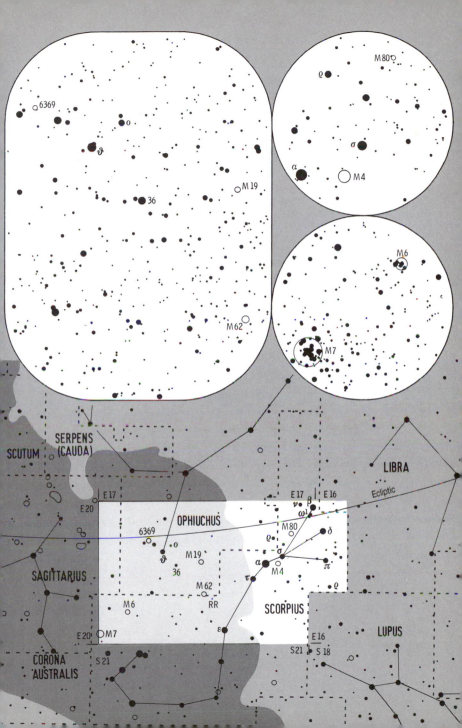

NEBULA		Const.	Mag.		Size	Shape	Type	Vis.	Dist.	R.A.	Dec.
6210		Her	10^m	4$\frac{m}{(5')}$	0$'$.3	D 3	Plan	bn	3000 ly	16^{h}44$\frac{1}{2}^m$	+23$°$.8
6572		Oph	9	2	0.2	D 2	Plan	Op	2000	18 12	+ 6.8
6633		Oph	5	8	20	m	Open	ey	1200	18 28	+ 6.6
IC 4756		Ser	5$\frac{1}{2}$	11	60	m	Open	op	1500	18 39	+ 5.4
6694	M26	Sct	8$\frac{1}{2}$	10	10	p	Open	bn	6000	18 45	− 9.4
6705	M11	Sct	6	8	12	r	Open	op	6000	18 51	− 6.3
6712		Sct	8$\frac{1}{2}$	8	5	IX	Glob	bn	20000	18 53	− 8.7

6210	faint star in binoculars, small greenish disk in a telescope
6572	stellar except at highest magnification, greenish
6633	quite bright, impressive irregular features, rewarding object
IC 4756	sparse, a few scattered stars, inconspicuous, best in binoculars
6694 M26	faint open cluster, in small telescopes still nebulous
6705 M11	bright glow in binoculars, slightly triangular, the impressive number of stars becomes apparent in large telescopes
6712	faint globular cluster, even in large telescopes barely resolved

STAR			Mag.	Spec.	Name, Comments	Dist.	R.A.	Dec.
7	κ	Her	4^m.7	d G9 III	. . . .	500 ly	16^{h}08^m.1	+17$°$.05
20	γ	Her	3.8	A9 III	. . . .	150	16 21.9	+19.15
27	β	Her	2.8	G8 III	Ruticulus	100	16 30.2	+21.49
64	α	Her	2.9–3.7 d M2 II		Rasalgethi	600	17 14.6	+14.39
65	δ	Her	3.1	A3 IV	. . . .	90	17 15.0	+24.84
86	μ	Her	3.4	G5 IV	. . . .	25	17 46.5	+27.72
92	ξ	Her	3.7	G9 III	. . . .	150	17 57.8	+29.25
95		Her	4.3	d F6 III	. . . .	300	18 01.5	+21.60
103	o	Her	3.8	B9 V	. . . .	150	18 07.5	+28.76
100		Her	5.1	d A3 V	. . . .	250	18 07.8	+26.10
58	η	Ser	3.3	K1 III	. . . .	60	18 21.3	− 2.90
109		Her	3.8	K2 III	. . . .	120	18 23.7	+21.77
59		Ser	4.8–5.7 d F9 III		d Serpentis	300	18 27.2	+ 0.20
	α	Sct	3.9	K3 III	. . . .	150	18 35.2	− 8.24
5		Aql	5.8	d A2 V	. . . .	300	18 46.5	− 0.96
	β	Sct	4.2	G5 II	. . . .	500	18 47.2	− 4.75
R		Sct	4.5–8.2	G7 Ib	. . . .	2500	18 47.5	− 5.70
63	ϑ	Ser	4.0	d A5 V	Alya	100	18 56.2	+ 4.20

BINARY			Mag.	Spec.	PA	Sep.	Vis.
7	κ	Her	5^m.0 6^m.3	G8 K1	13$°$	27$''$.5	Bn
64	α	Her	3–4 5.4	M5!G5	104	4.6	tl
95		Her	5.0 5.2	A5!G8	257	6.3	tl
100		Her	5.9 5.9	A3 A3	3	14.2	tl
59		Ser	5–6 7.6	G0 F0	319	3.7	tl
5		Aql	5.9 7.6	A2 F0	121	13.0	tl
63	ϑ	Ser	4.6 5.0	A5 A5	104	22.4	Bn

VARIABLE STAR

64 α Her semiregular
  Per. 50 d – 6 years
  binary magnitudes
  are 3^m.0–4^m.0 and 5^m.4
59 d Ser irregular
R Sct semiregular
  Period 140–146 d

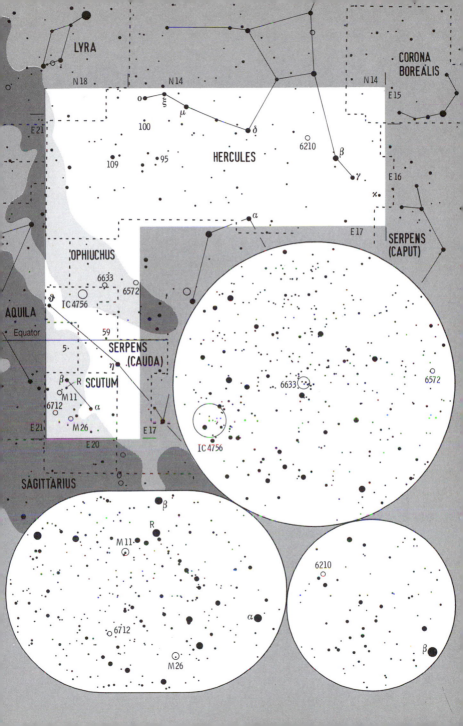

NEBULA		Const.	Mag.		Size	Shape	Type	Vis.	Dist.	R.A.	Dec.
6494	M23	Sgr	6^m	9$^m_{(5')}$	25$'$	m	Open	op	2500 ly	17^{h}57^m	−19$?$0
6514	M20	Sgr	7	10	25	Em2	Diff	Op	5000	18 03	−23.0
6523	M8	Sgr	5	10	60	Em4	Diff	ey	5000	18 04	−24.4
6531	M21	Sgr	6½	8	10	m	Open	op	4000	18 05	−22.5
	M24	Sgr	4	10	100	Milky	Way cl.	ey	5000	18 17	−18.5
6611	M16	Ser	6	9	25	Em2	Diff	op	6000	18 19	−13.8
6613	M18	Sgr	7½	9	10	p n	Open	Op	5000	18 20	−17.1
6618	M17	Sgr	6	10	40	Em2	Diff	op	5000	18 21	−16.2
6626	M28	Sgr	7	8	8	IV	Glob	op	20000	18 24½	−24.9
6637	M69	Sgr	8	8	5	V	Glob	Op	30000	18 31½	−32.3
IC 4725	M25	Sgr	5½	9	30	m	Open	Ey	2000	18 32	−19.2
6656	M22	Sgr	5	8	20	VII	Glob	ey	10000	18 36	−23.9
6681	M70	Sgr	8	8	5	V	Glob	Op	40000	18 43	−32.3
6715	M54	Sgr	8	8	6	III	Glob	Op	60000	18 55	−30.5

6494	M23	resolved in binoculars, impressive at low magnification
6514	M20	**Trifid Nebula**, division into three parts by three radial dust bands, structure visible in a telescope with nebular filter at low power
6523	M8	**Lagoon nebula**, visible to the unaided eye, fantastic nebula, especially through a nebular filter, star cluster in eastern part
6531	M21	resolved in binoculars, few bright stars, inconspicuous
	M24	according to Messier clearly the Milky Way cloud, not NGC 6603
6611	M16	**Eagle Nebula**, the cluster there is apparent without nebular filter
6613	M18	sparse, inconspicous since the surrounding field is quite rich
6618	M17	**Omega Nebula, Swan Nebula**, fantastic structure, bright arms, knots, and dark dust clouds, more detail with a nebular filter
6626	M28	asymmetric shape, bright central area, hard to resolve
6637	M69	faint, partially resolved in a large telescope, irregular outline
IC 4725	M25	very nicely resolved in binoculars, irregular stellar groups
6656	M22	very bright oval, impressive in large telescopes, uncountable stars
6681	M70	rather faint, distinct center, outer portion only just resolvable
6715	M54	almost impossible to resolve in amateur telescopes, high power

STAR			Mag.	Spec.	Name, Comments	Dist.	R.A.	Dec.
10	γ	Sgr	3^{m}0	K0 III	Alnasl	120 ly	18^{h}05^{m}8	−30$?$42
13	μ	Sgr	3.8	B8 Ia	. . . .	4000	18 13.8	−21.06
19	δ	Sgr	2.7	K2 III	Kaus Media	80	18 21.0	−29.83
20	ε	Sgr	1.8	B9 III	Kaus Australis . . .	100	18 24.2	−34.38
22	λ	Sgr	2.8	K2 III	Kaus Borealis . . .	100	18 28.0	−25.42
27	φ	Sgr	3.2	B8 III	. . . .	250	18 45.7	−26.99
34	σ	Sgr	2.0	B3 V	Nunki	200	18 55.3	−26.30
37	ξ^2	Sgr	3.5	K1 III	. . . .	150	18 57.7	−21.11
38	ζ	Sgr	2.6	A2 III	. . . .	100	19 02.6	−29.88
39	o	Sgr	3.8	G8 III	. . . .	120	19 04.7	−21.74
40	τ	Sgr	3.3	K1 III	. . . .	120	19 06.9	−27.67
41	π	Sgr	2.9	F2 II	. . . .	300	19 09.8	−21.02

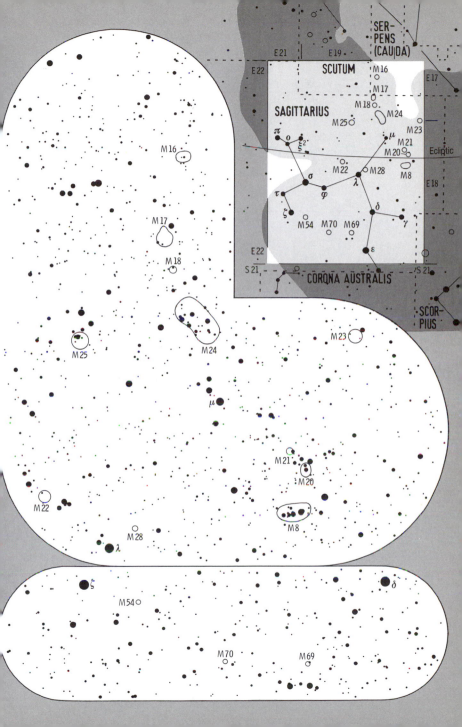

SER-
PENS
(CAUDA)

E 21   E 19

E 22

SCUTUM

M 16

M 17

E 17

M 18

SAGITTARIUS

M 24

M 25

M 23

π

o

ξ²

ξ

μ

M 21

Ecliptic

M 20

E 18

M 22

λ

M 28

M 8

σ

τ

φ

ζ

δ

γ

M 54   M 70   M 69

E 22

ε

S 21

S 21

CORONA AUSTRALIS

SCOR-
PIUS

M 16

M 17

M 18

M 24

M 25

M 23

M 22

μ

M 21

M 20

M 8

M 28

λ

M 54

ζ

δ

M 70

M 69

NEBULA	Const.	Mag.		Size	Shape	Type	Vis.	Dist.	R.A.	Dec.
6838 M71	Sge	$8\frac{1}{2}^m$	$9^m_{(5')}$	6'	Open?	Glob	bn	15 000 ly	19^h54^m	+18°8
6853 M27	Vul	8	8	8	A 4	Plan	Op	1 000	19 59½	+22.7

6838 M71	interesting features, triangular shape, resolved into stars in large telescopes, is it a globular cluster or very rich open cluster?
6853 M27	**Dumbbell Nebula,** may be the most beautiful planetary, shape visible in binoculars, more detail in telescopes

STAR		Mag.	Spec.	Name, Comments	Dist.	R.A.	Dec.
13	ε Aql	4.̇0	K2 III	. . . .	200 ly	$18^h59^m.6$	+15°.07
12	Aql	4.0	K1 III	. . . .	200	19 01.7	− 5.74
15	Aql	5.2	d K1 III	. . . .	500	19 05.0	− 4.03
17	ζ Aql	3.0	B9 V	. . . .	100	19 05.4	+13.86
16	λ Aql	3.4	B8 V	. . . .	100	19 06.2	− 4.88
R	Aql	5.6–12.0	M7 III	. . . .	800	19 06.4	+ 8.23
30	δ Aql	3.4	F1 IV	. . . .	50	19 25.5	+ 3.11
6	α Vul	4.4	M0 III	. . . .	300	19 28.7	+24.66
5	α Sge	4.4	G1 II	. . . .	600	19 40.1	+18.01
6	β Sge	4.4	G8 III	. . . .	300	19 41.0	+17.48
50	γ Aql	2.7	K3 II	Tarazed	300	19 46.3	+10.61
7	δ Sge	3.8	M2 II	. . . .	600	19 47.4	+18.53
52	π Aql	5.7	d A9 III	. . . .	500	19 48.7	+11.82
53	α Aql	0.8	A7 V	**Altair, Atair**	16	19 50.8	+ 8.87
55	η Aql	3.5–4.4	F8 Ib	. . . .	1 500	19 52.5	+ 1.01
57	Aql	5.3	d B7 V	. . . .	600	19 54.6	− 8.23
60	β Aql	3.7	G8 IV	Alshain	40	19 55.3	+ 6.41
12	γ Sge	3.5	K9 III	. . . .	200	19 58.8	+19.49
16	Vul	5.2	d F3 II	. . . .	800	20 02.0	+24.94
15	Sge	5.4	d F6 V	. . . .	60	20 04.1	+17.08
65	ϑ Aql	3.2	B9 III	. . . .	200	20 11.3	− 0.82
2	ε Del	4.0	B6 III	. . . .	500	20 33.2	+11.30
6	β Del	3.6	F5 IV	. . . .	80	20 37.5	+14.60
9	α Del	3.8	B9 IV	. . . .	200	20 39.6	+15.91
11	δ Del	4.4	A7 III	. . . .	200	20 43.5	+15.07
12	γ Del	3.9	d G6 IV	. . . .	80	20 46.7	+16.12

BINARY		Mag.	Spec.	PA	Sep.	Vis.
15	Aql	5.̇4 7.̇1	K1 K2 '90	210°	39.̇0	Bn
			2010	210	39.5	Bn
52	π Aql	6.2 6.9	F2 A2	106	1.4	Tl
57	Aql	5.7 6.5	B7 B8	170	35.7	Bn
16	Vul	5.8 6.2	F3 F	125	0.8	Tl
15	Sge	5.8 6.8	G1 A2	333	213	Op
12	γ Del	4.3 5.2	K0 F7 '90	268	9.4	tl
			2010	267	9.0	tl

VARIABLE STAR	
R Aql	Mira type
Period	≈ 285 d
Max.	≈ 2448005
Min.	phase 0.58
55 η Aql	Cepheid
Period	7.17664 d
Max.	2447897.4
Min.	phase 0.68

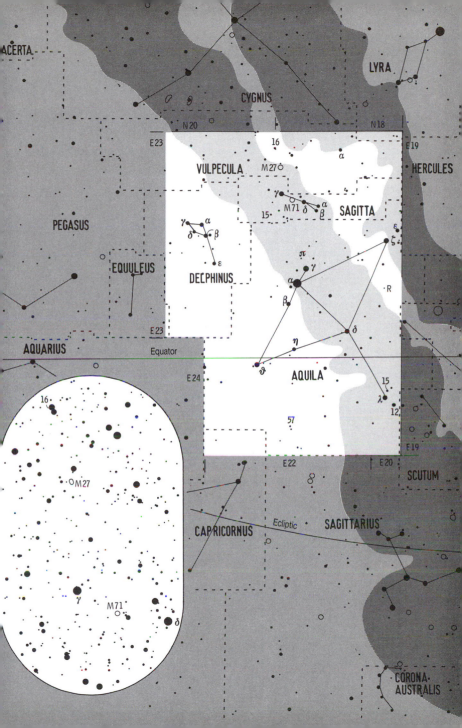

NEBULA	Const.	Mag.		Size	Shape	Type	Vis.	Dist.	R.A.	Dec.
6809 M55	Sgr	7^m	10$^m_{(5')}$	15$'$	XI	Glob	op	20 000 ly	19^{h}40^m	−31°0
6818	Sgr	10	4	0.4	R 3	Plan	bn	5000	19 44	−14.2
6822	Sgr	9	10	10	Ir 3	Galx	Bn	1.5 M	19 45	−14.8
6864 M75	Sgr	8½	8	4	I	Glob	bn	60 000	20 06	−21.9
7099 M30	Cap	7½	9	8	V	Glob	Op	30 000	21 40½	−23.2

6809 M55	quite large glow in binoculars, completely resolved in large telescopes, irregular outline, difficult to find
6818	stellar in binoculars, oval disk at high magnification, greenish color visible in a large telescope
6822	**Barnard's Galaxy,** closer to us than the Andromeda Galaxy, very hard to see since there is no detail, not even a core visible, darkest sky and lowest power essential
6864 M75	quite distant globular cluster, therefore faint, small, and not resolvable into individual stars, extraordinary bright center
7099 M30	distinct center, elongated envelope, outer portions can be resolved into stars in large telescopes

STAR		Mag.	Spec.	Name, Comments	Dist.	R.A.	Dec.
44	ϱ^1 Sgr	3^{m}9	F 0 IV	. . . .	90 ly	19^{h}21^{m}7	−17°85
5	α^1 Cap	4.2	G3 Ib	Algiedi ⎫ Sep. 6$'$4	1500	20 17.6	−12.51
6	α^2 Cap	3.6	G9 III	Algiedi ⎭	120	20 18.1	−12.55
9	β Cap	3.0	d F 7 III	. . . .	100	20 21.0	−14.78
11	ϱ Cap	4.6	d F 5 IV	. . . .	100	20 28.9	−17.82
12	o Cap	5.5	d A 4 V	. . . .	250	20 29.9	−18.58
16	ψ Cap	4.1	F 4 V	. . . .	35	20 46.1	−25.27
18	ω Cap	4.1	K5 III	. . . .	300	20 51.8	−26.92
23	ϑ Cap	4.1	A1 V	. . . .	150	21 05.9	−17.23
32	ι Cap	4.3	G8 III	. . . .	200	21 22.2	−16.83
34	ζ Cap	3.7	G4 Ib	. . . .	1500	21 26.7	−22.41
40	γ Cap	3.7	F 0 IV	. . . .	100	21 40.1	−16.66
49	δ Cap	2.8–3.1	A9 V	Deneb Algedi . . .	40	21 47.0	−16.13
12	η PsA	5.4	d B 8 V	. . . .	500	22 00.8	−28.45
17	β PsA	4.3	d A 1 V	. . . .	150	22 31.5	−32.35
18	ε PsA	4.2	B 8 V	. . . .	250	22 40.7	−27.04
22	γ PsA	4.4	A 0 IV	. . . .	200	22 52.5	−32.88
23	δ PsA	4.2	G7 III	. . . .	150	22 55.9	−32.54
24	α PsA	1.2	A 3 V	**Fomalhaut**	22	22 57.6	−29.62

BINARY		Mag.	Spec.	PA	Sep.	Vis.
9	β Cap	3^{m}1 6^{m}1	F8 A0	267°	205$''$	Op
11	ϱ Cap	4.8 6.6	F2 K1	150	257	op
12	o Cap	5.9 6.7	A3 A6	239	21.9	Bn
12	η PsA	5.8 6.8	B7 A2	115	1.8	tl
17	β PsA	4.3 7.8	A0!G2	172	30.3	tl

VARIABLE STAR

49 δ Cap   Algol type
     Period   1.02277 d
     Min.   2447893.32
     Max. ph.0.04–0.96
     light curve varies

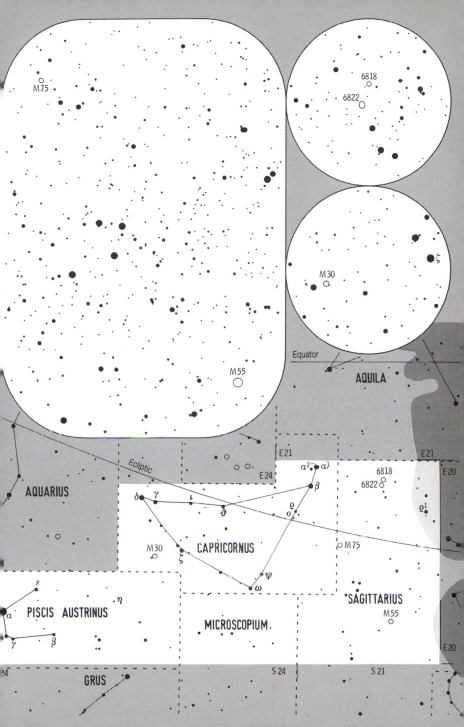

M75

6818
6822

6818
6822

ζ

M30

M55

Equator

AQUILA

Ecliptic

E 21

E 24

E 21

E 20

α² α¹
β

6818
6822

E 20

ϱ¹

AQUARIUS

δ γ ι
ϑ

ϱ
σ

M30
ζ

CAPRICORNUS

M75

ε

η

M55

α

PISCIS AUSTRINUS

ψ
ω

SAGITTARIUS

γ β

MICROSCOPIUM

S 24

S 21

E 20

GRUS

NEBULA		Const.	Mag.	Size	Shape	Type	Vis.	Dist.	R.A.	Dec.
7078	M15	Peg	$6\frac{1}{2}^m$ $8^m_{(5')}$	$10'$	IV	Glob	op	30000ly	21^h30^m	$+12°2$
7331		Peg	$9\frac{1}{2}$ 10	10	Sb 7	Galx	Bn	40 M	22 37	+34.4

7078	M15	relatively easy to find and to see, slightly oval, resolved in a large telescope with the exception of the bright center
7331		a spindle with a fine elongated central area is visible in telescopes

STAR			Mag.	Spec.	Name, Comments	Dist.	R.A.	Dec.
1	ε	Equ	5.1^m	d F 6 IV	. . . .	150ly	20^h59^m1	$+ 4.29$
5	γ	Equ	4.7	F 0 IV	. . . .	120	21 10.3	+10.13
7	δ	Equ	4.5	F 7 V	. . . .	55	21 14.5	+10.01
8	α	Equ	3.9	G0 III	Kitalphar	150	21 15.8	+ 5.25
1		Peg	4.1	K1 III	. . . .	200	21 22.1	+19.80
8	ε	Peg	2.4	K2 Ib	Enif	500	21 44.2	+ 9.88
10	κ	Peg	4.1	F 5 IV	. . . .	90	21 44.6	+25.65
24	ι	Peg	3.8	F 5 V	. . . .	40	22 07.0	+25.35
29	π	Peg	4.3	F 5 II	also designated π^2 Peg	300	22 10.0	+33.18
26	ϑ	Peg	3.5	A2 V	Baham	80	22 10.2	+ 6.20
37		Peg	5.5	d F 4 IV	. . . .	150	22 30.0	+ 4.43
42	ζ	Peg	3.4	B8 V	Homam	150	22 41.5	+10.83
44	η	Peg	2.9	G2 II	Matar	200	22 43.0	+30.22
47	λ	Peg	4.0	G8 III	. . . .	100	22 46.5	+23.57
46	ξ	Peg	4.2	F 7 IV	. . . .	60	22 46.7	+12.17
48	μ	Peg	3.5	G9 III	Sadalbari	120	22 50.0	+24.60
53	β	Peg	2.3–2.7	M2 II	**Scheat**	200	23 03.8	+28.08
4	β	Psc	4.5	B6 V	. . . .	300	23 03.9	+ 3.82
54	α	Peg	2.5	B9 V	**Markab**	100	23 04.8	+15.21
6	γ	Psc	3.7	G9 III	Homam	120	23 17.2	+ 3.28
10	ϑ	Psc	4.3	K1 III	. . . .	250	23 28.0	+ 6.38
72		Peg	5.0	d K4 III	. . . .	600	23 34.0	+31.33
17	ι	Psc	4.1	F 7 V	. . . .	45	23 39.9	+ 5.63
18	λ	Psc	4.5	A7 V	. . . .	90	23 42.0	+ 1.78
19		Psc	4.8–5.2	C5 II	TX Piscium	2000	23 46.4	+ 3.49
28	ω	Psc	4.0	F 4 IV	. . . .	120	23 59.3	+ 6.86

BINARY			Mag.	Spec.		PA	Sep.	Vis.
1	ε	Equ	5.8^m 6.1^m	F 5	F 7 '90	285°	$1.0''$	Tl
					2000	284	0.8	Tl
					2010	283	0.5	-
			7.1		G0	68	10.7	tl
37		Peg	5.8 7.1	F 4	F 5 '90	118	0.9	Tl
					2000	118	0.7	-
					2010	119	0.5	-
72		Peg	5.7 5.8	K4	K5 '90	89	0.5	-
					2010	105	0.5	-

VARIABLE STAR

53 β Peg irregular
19 TX Psc irregular
reddish giant,
among the largest
of known stars,
diameter approx.
1 000 000 000 km,
600 000 000 miles,
700 solar diameters

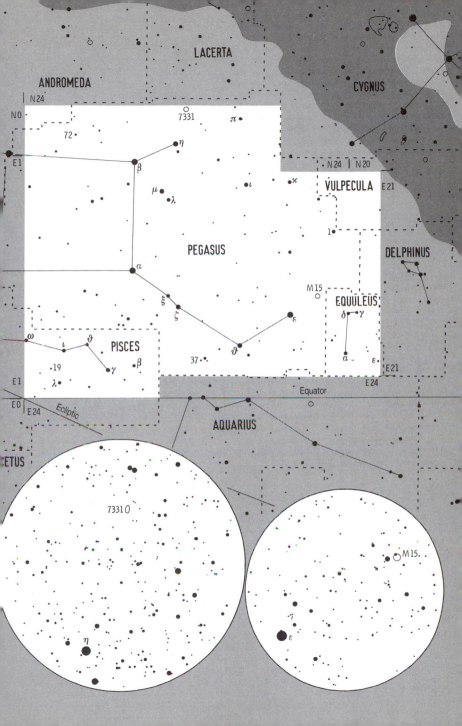

NEBULA	Const.	Mag.		Size	Shape		Type	Vis.	Dist.	R.A.	Dec.
6981 M72	Aqr	$9\tfrac{1}{2}^{m}$	$9^{m}_{(5')}$	4$'$	IX		Glob	bn	60000 ly	$20^{h}53\tfrac{1}{2}^{m}$	$-12\overset{\circ}{.}5$
6994 M73	Aqr	8½	7	2.5	p		Open	Op	2000	20 59	−12.6
7009	Aqr	9	4	0.6	A	3	Plan	Op	2500	21 04	−11.4
7089 M2	Aqr	6½	8	10	II		Glob	op	40000	21 33½	− 0.8
7293	Aqr	7	9	15	R	2	Plan	op	500	22 30	−20.8

6981	M72	faintest globular cluster in this atlas, not resolvable
6994	M73	Messier accurately describes it as a group of 3–4 stars
7009		**Saturn Nebula**, beautiful features in a large telescope at high power, elliptical, greenish, faint $11\tfrac{1}{2}^{m}$ central star
7089	M2	large bright glow in binoculars, quite difficult to resolve
7293		**Helix Nebula**, brightest and nearest planetary, hard unless sky conditions are perfect, rich features with a nebular filter

STAR		Mag.	Spec.	Name, Comments	Dist.	R.A.	Dec.
2	ε Aqr	$3\overset{m}{.}8$	A1 V	. . . .	120 ly	$20^{h}47\overset{m}{.}7$	− 9$\overset{\circ}{.}$50
12	Aqr	5.5	d G9 III	. . . .	500	21 04.1	− 5.82
13	ν Aqr	4.5	G8 III	. . . .	250	21 09.6	−11.37
22	β Aqr	2.9	G0 Ib	Sadalsuud	1000	21 31.6	− 5.57
34	α Aqr	3.0	G2 Ib	Sadalmelik	1000	22 05.8	− 0.32
41	Aqr	5.3	d G7 III	. . . .	400	22 14.3	−21.07
48	γ Aqr	3.8	A0 V	Sadachbia	100	22 21.7	− 1.39
55	ζ Aqr	3.7	d F3 IV	. . . .	100	22 28.8	− 0.02
62	η Aqr	4.0	B8 V	. . . .	150	22 35.4	− 0.12
71	τ² Aqr	4.0	M0 III	. . . .	250	22 49.6	−13.59
73	λ Aqr	3.8	M2 III	. . . .	250	22 52.6	− 7.58
76	δ Aqr	3.3	A3 IV	. . . .	100	22 54.6	−15.82
88	Aqr	3.7	K0 III	. . . .	150	23 09.4	−21.17
94	Aqr	5.1	d G6 IV	. . . .	80	23 19.1	−13.46
98	Aqr	4.0	K0 III	. . . .	120	23 23.0	−20.10
101	Aqr	4.7	d A0 II	. . . .	1000	23 33.3	−20.91
104	Aqr	4.7	d G0 II	. . . .	1000	23 41.8	−17.81
R	Aqr	5.8–12.4	M7 III	. . . .	1000	23 43.8	−15.28
107	Aqr	5.3	d F1 IV	. . . .	200	23 46.0	−18.68

BINARY		Mag.		Spec.		PA	Sep.	Vis.
12	Aqr	$5\overset{m}{.}8$	$7\overset{m}{.}3$	G4!	A3	192°	2$\overset{''}{.}$8	tl
41	Aqr	5.6	7.1	K0	F5	112	5.0	tl
55 ζ	Aqr	4.3	4.5	F3	F4 '90	208	1.9	tl
					2000	192	2.1	tl
					2010	180	2.4	tl
94	Aqr	5.3	7.3	G5	K2	351	12.6	tl
101	Aqr	4.8	7.1	A0	A	126	1.2	Tl
104	Aqr	4.8	7.6	G0	F	6	113	bn
107	Aqr	5.7	6.7	F1	F2	135	6.8	tl

VARIABLE STAR

R Aqr	Mira type
Period	387 d
Max.	2448202
Min.	phase 0.58
Mean	$6\overset{m}{.}5$–$10\overset{m}{.}3$

period increases
and decreases
slightly in a
24-year-long cycle

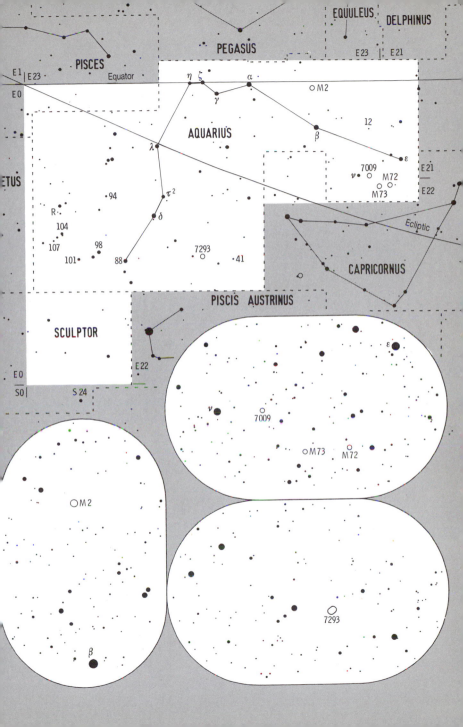

NEBULA	Const.	Mag.		Size	Shape	Type	Vis.	Dist.	R.A.	Dec.
55	Scl	8^m	10$^m_{(5')}$	25'	Sm8	Galx	Op	8 Mly	0^{h}15^m	−39°.2
104	Tuc	4	7	25	III	Glob	ey	15000	0 24	−72.1
292 SMC	Tuc	2½	10	180	Sm4	Galx	ey	200000	0 53	−72.8
362	Tuc	6½	8	10	III	Glob	Ey	30000	1 03	−70.9
1291	Eri	9	9	6	Sa 4	Galx	bn	30 M	3 17	−41.1
1316	For	9½	9	4	L 3	Galx	bn	60 M	3 23	−37.2
1365	For	10	10	8	Sb 5	Galx	Bn	60 M	3 33½	−36.1

55		very elongated and slightly asymmetric, needs low power
104		**47 Tucanae**, majestic globular cluster, even with unaided eye
292	SMC	**Small Magellanic Cloud**, eye-catching under dark sky with unaided eye, features in northern portion, low power necessary
362		bright distinct center, edges resolved in large telescopes
1291		round central area, hardly any features in amateur telescopes
1316		**Fornax A**, brightest galaxy of the **Fornax Cluster**, stellar core
1365		bar of the barred spiral barely visible, many 11^m galaxies nearby

STAR		Mag.	Spec.	Name, Comments	Dist.	R.A.	Dec.
ε	Phe	3.9	K0 III	. . . .	70 ly	0^{h}09^m.4	−45°.75
β	Hyi	2.8	G1 IV	. . . .	20	0 25.8	−77.25
κ	Phe	3.9	A5 V	. . . .	60	0 26.2	−43.68
α	Phe	2.4	K0 III	Ankaa	80	0 26.3	−42.31
β	Tuc	3.7	d A1 V	. . . .	150	0 31.6	−62.96
β	Phe	3.3	d G8 III	. . . .	150	1 06.1	−46.72
ζ	Phe	3.9–4.3	d B8 V	. . . .	250	1 08.4	−55.25
γ	Phe	3.4	K6 II	. . . .	300	1 28.4	−43.32
δ	Phe	4.0	K0 III	. . . .	100	1 31.3	−49.07
α	Eri	0.5	B4 V	**Achernar**	90	1 37.7	−57.24
p	Eri	5.1	d K3 V	. . . .	21	1 39.8	−56.20
χ	Eri	3.7	G6 IV	. . . .	50	1 56.0	−51.61
α	Hyi	2.9	F0 V	. . . .	45	1 58.8	−61.57
φ	Eri	3.6	B8 V	. . . .	120	2 16.5	−51.51
ι	Eri	4.1	K0 III	. . . .	200	2 40.7	−39.86
R	Hor	4.7–14.3	M7 III	. . . .	500	2 53.9	−49.89
ϑ	Eri	3.0	d A3 III	Acamar	120	2 58.3	−40.30
f	Eri	4.3	d A0 V	. . . .	200	3 48.6	−37.62

BINARY		Mag.		Spec.		PA	Sep.	Vis.
β	Tuc	4.4	4.5	B9	A4	168°	27".1	Bn
β	Phe	4.0	4.2	G8	G	325	1.6	tl
ζ	Phe	4	6.9	B6!	F7	243	6.4	tl
p	Eri	5.8	5.9	K5	K0 '90	193	11.3	tl
					2010	188	11.6	tl
ϑ	Eri	3.3	4.4	A4	A1	90	8.2	tl
f	Eri	4.8	5.4	B9	A1	216	8.1	tl

VARIABLE STAR

ζ Phe   Algol type
Period 1.669767 d
Min. 2447893.63
Max. ph.0.06–0.94
R Hor   Mira type
Period   405 d
Max. ≈ 2447975

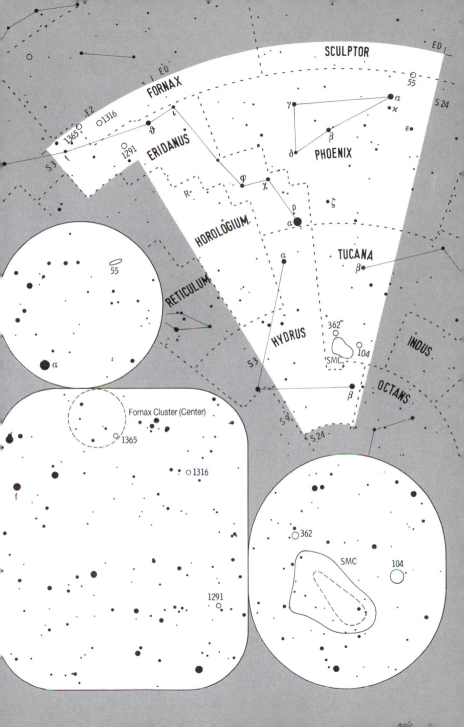

SCULPTOR

FORNAX

E0

E2

1365 ○ ○1316

1365

ϑ

f

1291

ERIDANUS

R

φ

χ

ρ

α

HOROLOGIUM

S 3

E0

E0

55

α

χ

γ

δ

β

ε

PHOENIX

ζ

S 24

TUCANA

β

α

RETICULUM

55

α

α

HYDRUS

362"

104

SMC

INDUS

S 3

β

OCTANS

S 9

S 24

Fornax Cluster (Center)

1365

1316

f

1291

362

SMC

104

NEBULA	Const.	Mag.		Size	Shape	Type	Vis.	Dist.	R.A.	Dec.
1851	Col	$7\frac{1}{2}^m$	$8^m_{(5')}$	6'	II	Glob	op	40000 ly	5^h14^m	−40°0
	LMC	Dor	$0\frac{1}{2}$ 10	480	Sm2	Galx	ey	150000	5 24	−69.8
2070		Dor	5 8	25	Em2	Diff	ey	150000	5 39	−69.1
2516		Car	4 8	40	r	Open	ey	2000	7 58	−60.9

1851	central condensation well visible in binoculars, hardly resolvable
LMC	**Large Magellanic Cloud**, brightest and largest nebula, bar and traces of spiral arms with unaided eye, in binoculars under dark sky past all description, and still better in telescopes
2070	**Tarantula Nebula**, fantastic, unique, 5000 times as luminous as the Orion Nebula, supernova 1987A remnant 20' southwest
2516	easy with unaided eye, impressively rich in binoculars

STAR		Mag.	Spec.	Name, Comments	Dist.	R.A.	Dec.
β	Ret	3.9^m	K0 IV	. . . .	60 ly	$3^h44^m_{.}2$	−64°81
γ	Hyi	3.2	M1 III	. . . .	150	3 47.2	−74.24
δ	Ret	4.6	M2 III	. . . .	300	3 58.7	−61.40
α	Hor	3.9	K1 III	. . . .	200	4 14.0	−42.29
α	Ret	3.4	G7 II	. . . .	400	4 14.4	−62.47
γ	Dor	4.3	F 3 V	. . . .	70	4 16.0	−51.49
ε	Ret	4.4	K3 IV	. . . .	70	4 16.5	−59.30
α	Dor	3.3	A0 III	. . . .	200	4 35.0	−55.05
ι	Pic	5.2	d F 0 IV	. . . .	200	4 50.9	−53.46
β	Dor	3.5–4.1	F 8 Ia	. . . .	8000	5 33.6	−62.49
β	Pic	3.9	A5 V	. . . .	80	5 47.3	−51.07
γ	Pic	4.5	K1 III	. . . .	250	5 49.8	−56.17
η	Col	4.0	K0 III	. . . .	150	5 59.1	−42.82
α	Car	−0.7	F 0 Ib	**Canopus**	150	6 24.0	−52.70
ν	Pup	3.2	B 8 III	. . . .	250	6 37.8	−43.20
α	Pic	3.3	A6 V	. . . .	60	6 48.2	−61.94
τ	Pup	2.9	K0 III	. . . .	80	6 49.9	−50.61
γ	Vol	3.6	d G7 III	. . . .	150	7 08.8	−70.50
δ	Vol	4.0	F 8 Ib	. . . .	2000	7 16.8	−67.96
ζ	Vol	3.9	K0 III	. . . .	200	7 41.8	−72.61
χ	Car	3.5	B 2 IV	. . . .	600	7 56.8	−52.98
κ	Vol	4.8	d B 9 III	. . . .	500	8 19.9	−71.51
ε	Car	1.9	K0 III	**Avior**	150	8 22.5	−59.51
β	Vol	3.8	K2 III	. . . .	150	8 25.7	−66.14
c	Car	3.8	B 8 II	. . . .	500	8 55.0	−60.64
α	Vol	4.0	A4 V	. . . .	80	9 02.4	−66.40

BINARY		Mag.	Spec.	PA	Sep.	Vis.
ι	Pic	5.6^m 6.4^m	F 0 F 2	58°	12."3	tl
γ	Vol	3.8 5.7	G9 F 2	300	13.6	tl
κ	Vol	5.4 5.7	B 9 A 0	57	65	bn

VARIABLE STAR

β Dor		Cepheid
	Period	9.842 d
	Max.	2447893.4

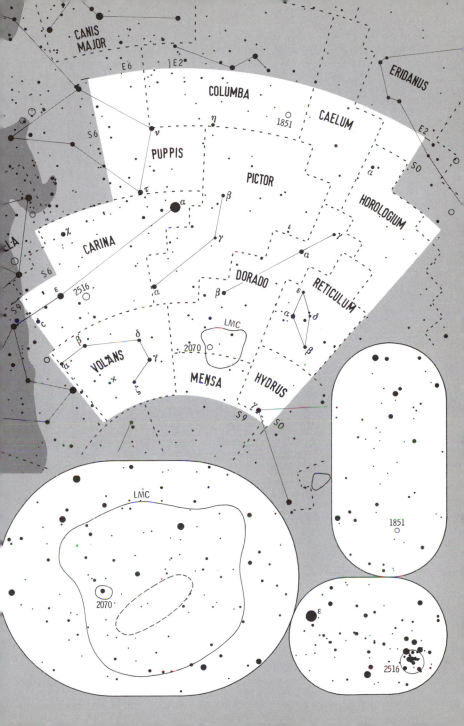

NEBULA	Const.	Mag.		Size	Shape	Type	Vis.	Dist.	R.A.	Dec.
2451	Pup	$3\frac{1}{2}^m$	$8^m_{(5')}$	40'	p	Open	ey	1500 ly	7^h45^m	$-38°.0$
2477	Pup	6	9	25	r	Open	op	5000	7 52	-38.5
2547	Vel	5	7	15	m n	Open	ey	2000	8 11	-49.3
2546	Pup	6	10	30	m	Open	op	3000	8 12	-37.6
IC 2391	Vel	3	8	40	p	Open	ey	500	8 40	-53.1
3132	Vel	9	5	1.0	R 3	Plan	bn	2000	10 07	-40.4
3201	Vel	7	9	12	X	Glob	op	15000	10 18	-46.4

2451	nicely resolved in binoculars, few stars but very bright ones
2477	tremendous number of stars, nicely resolved in a telescope
2547	bright open cluster for binoculars, not as much for telescopes
2546	elongated cluster in binoculars, inconspicuous in a telescope
IC 2391	o (omikron) **Velorum Cluster**, for unaided eye to binoculars, sparse
3132	oval disk with central star 10^m in a telescope
3201	irregular stellar condensations, resolved in a large telescope

STAR		Mag.	Spec.	Name, Comments	Dist.	R.A.	Dec.
L^2	Pup	$2^m_.6$–$6^m_.2$	M5 III	. . . .	150 ly	$7^h13^m_.5$	$-44°.64$
π	Pup	2.7	K4 III	. . . .	120	7 17.1	-37.10
υ	Pup	4.1	d B3 IV	also designated y Pup	800	7 18.4	-36.74
σ	Pup	3.3	K5 III	. . . .	150	7 29.2	-43.30
c	Pup	3.6	K2 Ib	in NGC 2451	1500	7 45.3	-37.97
a	Pup	3.7	K0 III	. . . .	250	7 52.2	-40.58
ζ	Pup	2.3	O5 Ia	. . . .	2000	8 03.6	-40.00
γ	Vel	1.5–1.7 d O7 Ia		Suhail Al Muhlif . .	1500	8 09.5	-47.34
o	Vel	3.6	B3 IV	in IC 2391	500	8 40.3	-52.92
b	Vel	3.8	F 2 Ia	. . . .	6000	8 40.6	-46.65
d	Vel	4.0	G5 III	. . . .	150	8 44.4	-42.65
δ	Vel	2.0	d A1 V	. . . .	70	8 44.7	-54.71
a	Vel	3.9	A0 III	. . . .	250	8 46.0	-46.04
c	Vel	3.8	K2 III	. . . .	200	9 04.2	-47.10
λ	Vel	2.2	K5 Ib	Suhail Al Wazn . .	500	9 08.0	-43.43
κ	Vel	2.5	B2 IV	. . . .	400	9 22.1	-55.01
ψ	Vel	3.6	F2 IV	. . . .	60	9 30.7	-40.47
φ	Vel	3.5	B5 Ib	. . . .	2500	9 56.9	-54.57
q	Vel	3.9	A2 V	. . . .	100	10 14.7	-42.12
p	Vel	3.8	F4 IV	. . . .	80	10 37.3	-48.23
x	Vel	4.1	d F9 II	. . . .	600	10 39.3	-55.60
μ	Vel	2.7	G5 III	. . . .	100	10 46.8	-49.42

BINARY		Mag.	Spec.	PA	Sep.	Vis.
υ	Pup	$4^m_.7$ $5^m_.1$	B3 B3	97°	240''	Ey
γ	Vel	2 4.2	O7 B1	220	41.2	Bn
δ	Vel	2.0 5.1	A0 F5	135	2.5	Tl
x	Vel	4.3 6.2	G2!B8	105	51.9	bn

VARIABLE STAR

L^2 Pup   semiregular
   Period   140.5 d
   Max. $\approx$ 2447980
γ Vel   Period $\approx$ 2 min.!

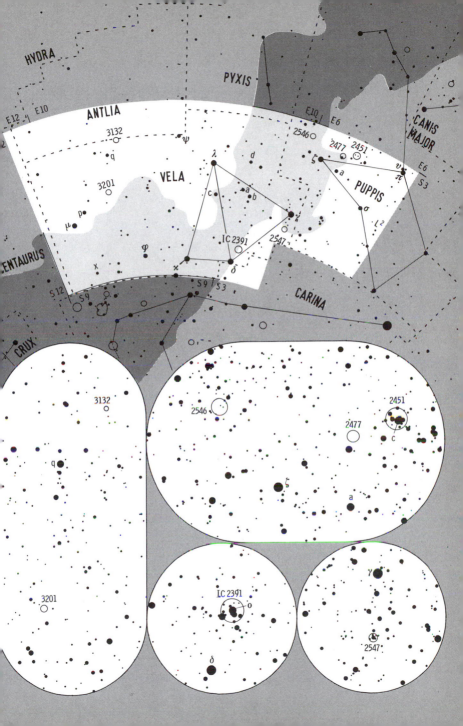

NEBULA	Const.	Mag.		Size	Shape	Type	Vis.	Dist.	R.A.	Dec.
2808	Car	$6\frac{1}{2}^m$	$7^m_{(5')}$	8′	I	Glob	Ey	30000 ly	9^h12^m	−64°9
3114	Car	$4\frac{1}{2}$	8	30	r	Open	ey	2500	10 03	−60.1
3293	Car	$5\frac{1}{2}$	6	6	m n	Open	ey	5000	10 36	−58.2
IC 2602	Car	2	7	60	m	Open	ey	800	10 43	−64.4
3372	Car	3	10	100	Em1	Diff	ey	6000	10 44	−59.9
3532	Car	$3\frac{1}{2}$	9	60	r	Open	ey	1500	11 06	−58.7

2808	resolved in a telescope, shape I = extreme central condensation
3114	impressive open cluster, rewarding in binoculars and telescopes
3293	small glow in binoculars, resolved in telescopes, takes high power
IC 2602	**Southern Pleiades**, similar to the Pleiades, only a little fainter
3372	η **Carinae Nebula**, conspicuous with unaided eye, full of features in binoculars, even better in a telescope at low power
3532	extremely rich, elongated, impressive in binoculars

STAR		Mag.	Spec.	Name, Comments	Dist.	R.A.	Dec.
α	Cha	4^m1	F 6 IV	. . . .	80 ly	8^h18^m5	−76°92
b¹	Car	4.7	d B 4 IV	. . . .	1000	8 57.0	−59.23
a	Car	3.4	B 2 IV	. . . .	600	9 11.0	−58.97
i	Car	4.0	B 3 III	. . . .	800	9 11.3	−62.32
β	Car	1.7	A 1 III	Miaplacidus	80	9 13.2	−69.72
ι	Car	2.3	A 9 Ib	. . . .	800	9 17.1	−59.28
N	Vel	3.1	K 5 III	. . . .	150	9 31.2	−57.03
R	Car	3.9–10.3	M 6 III	. . . .	500	9 32.2	−62.79
l	Car	3.3–4.2	G 5 Ib	ZZ Carinae	1500	9 45.2	−62.51
υ	Car	3.0	d A 8 Ib	. . . .	1000	9 47.1	−65.07
ω	Car	3.3	B 8 III	. . . .	250	10 13.7	−70.04
q	Car	3.4	K 4 II	. . . .	600	10 17.1	−61.33
I	Car	3.9	d F 1 IV	. . . .	60	10 24.4	−74.02
s	Car	3.8	F 1 II	. . . .	500	10 27.9	−58.74
p	Car	3.3	B 3 V	. . . .	300	10 32.0	−61.69
γ	Cha	4.1	M 0 III	. . . .	250	10 35.5	−78.61
ϑ	Car	2.8	B 0 V	in IC 2602	800	10 43.0	−64.39
δ	Cha	4.1	d A 3 IV	. . . .	800	10 45.6	−80.52
u	Car	3.7	d K 0 III	. . . .	70	10 53.5	−58.86
x	Car	3.9	G 2 Ia	in NGC 3532	5000	11 08.6	−58.97
ε	Cha	4.7	d B 9 V	. . . .	300	11 59.7	−78.22

BINARY		Mag.		Spec.		PA	Sep.	Vis.
b¹	Car	4^m9	6^m7	B 3	B 9	75°	40″3	Bn
υ	Car	3.1	6.0	A 8	A 8	127	5.0	tl
I	Car	4.0	6.2	F 2	A 2	22	233	op
δ	Cha	4.5	5.5	B 3!	K 0	343	265	Ey
u	Car	3.8	6.3	K 0!	B 3	204	157	Op
ε	Cha	4.9	6.5	B 9	A 0	38	135	Op

VARIABLE STAR

R Car	Mira type
Period	308.7 d
Max.	2448174
l ZZ Car	Cepheid
Period	35.53 d
Max.	2447915

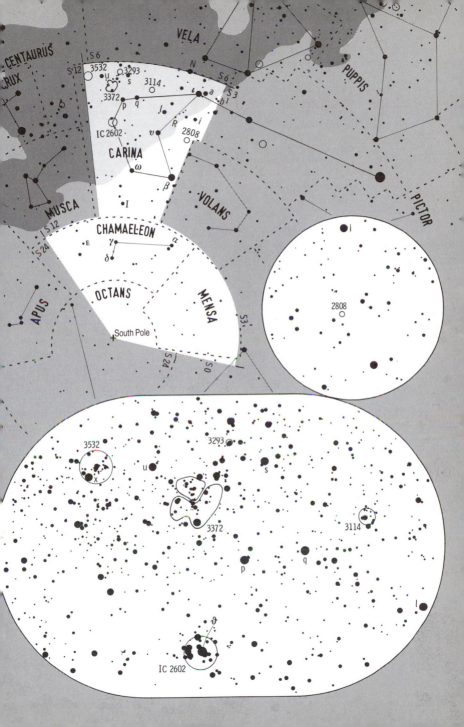

NEBULA	Const.	Mag.	Size	Shape	Type	Vis.	Dist.	R.A.	Dec.
3766	Cen	5^m $7^m_{(5')}$	$12'$	m	Open	ey	1500 ly	11^h36^m	$-61°6$
Coalsack	Cru	(3) (12)	360		Dark Nebula	ey	3000	12 52	−63.3
4755	Cru	5 6	10	m	Open	ey	6000	12 54	−60.3

3766	resolved in binoculars, wonderful in a telescope, interesting shape
Coalsack	most spectacular dark nebula, rich detail in binoculars
4755	**Jewel Box, κ Crucis Cluster**, resolved in binoculars, impressive in telescopes, arrow shaped, takes high magnification

STAR	Mag.	Spec.	Name, Comments	Dist.	R.A.	Dec.
π Cen	3^m9	B 5 V	. . . .	300 ly	11^h21^m0	$-54°49$
o Cen	4.3–4.6 d	F 2 Ia	. . . .	8000	11 31.8	−59.48
λ Cen	3.1	B 9 III	. . . .	200	11 35.8	−63.02
λ Mus	3.6	A 6 V	. . . .	50	11 45.6	−66.73
δ Cen	2.4	d B 2 IV	. . . .	500	12 08.3	−50.71
ρ Cen	4.0	B 4 V	. . . .	400	12 11.7	−52.37
δ Cru	2.8	B 2 V	. . . .	400	12 15.1	−58.75
ε Mus	4.0–4.3	M5 III	. . . .	100	12 17.6	−67.96
ζ Cru	4.0	B 3 V	. . . .	500	12 18.4	−64.00
ε Cru	3.4–4.0	K3 III	. . . .	150	12 21.4	−60.40
α Cru	0.8	d B 1 IV	**Acrux**	400	12 26.6	−63.10
σ Cen	3.9	B 3 V	. . . .	400	12 28.0	−50.23
γ Cru	1.6	d M3 III	Gacrux	120	12 31.2	−57.11
γ Mus	3.9	B 5 V	. . . .	200	12 32.5	−72.13
α Mus	2.7	B 3 IV	. . . .	300	12 37.2	−69.14
τ Cen	3.9	A 2 V	. . . .	100	12 37.7	−48.54
γ Cen	2.2	d A0 IV	. . . .	150	12 41.5	−48.96
β Mus	3.1	d B 2 V	. . . .	300	12 46.3	−68.11
β Cru	1.3	B 0 III	Mimosa	400	12 47.7	−59.69
μ Cru	3.7	d B 3 IV	. . . .	600	12 54.6	−57.18
δ Mus	3.6	K2 III	. . . .	200	13 02.3	−71.55

BINARY	Mag.		Spec.		PA	Sep.	Vis.
o Cen	5^m	5^m2	G2!	A 2	176°	265″	Ey
δ Cen	2.6	4.5	B 2	B 5	325	269	Ey
		6.4		B 9	223	198	Op
α Cru	1.4	1.8	B 1	B 2	112	4.0	tl
		4.9		B 4	202	90	bn
γ Cru	1.6	6.4	M3!	A 3	25	128	Bn
γ Cen	2.9	2.9	A 0	A 0 '90	353	1.4	Tl
				2000	347	1.0	Tl
				2005	341	0.7	-
				2010	324	0.4	-
β Mus	3.7	4.0	B 2	B 3	43	1.3	Tl
μ Cru	4.0	5.2	B 2	B 5	17	34.9	Bn

VARIABLE STAR

o Cen	semiregular
	Period ≈ 200 d ?
	Magnitudes:
	primary 4^m9–5^m4
	companion 5^m2
	two giants with
	different colors,
	very distant
ε Mus	semiregular
	Period ≈ 40 d
ε Cru	irregular ?
	Mean ≈ 3^m6

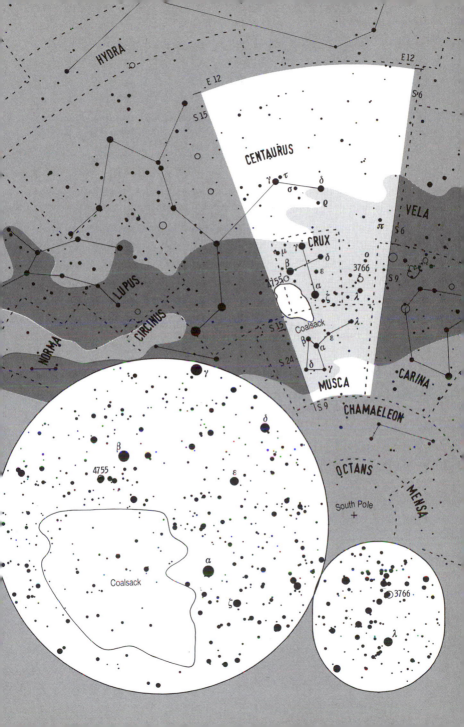

NEBULA	Const.	Mag.	Size	Shape	Type	Vis.	Dist.	R.A.	Dec.
5128	Cen	7^m $9_{(5')}$	12'	L 2	Galx	op	15 Mly	$13^h25\frac{1}{2}^m$	$-43^\circ0$
5139	Cen	$3\frac{1}{2}$ 7	30	VIII	Glob	ey	15000	13 27	-47.5
5460	Cen	6 10	30	p	Open	op	2000	14 08	-48.3
5822	Lup	$6\frac{1}{2}$ 11	40	r	Open	op	2500	15 05	-54.3

5128	**Centaurus A**, round glow in a small telescope, becomes remarkable in a large telescope, wide dark dust band with features
5139	ω **Centauri**, the primary of all globular clusters in the sky, easy with unaided eye, bright elliptical glow in binoculars, fantastic richness of stars in larger telescopes, fascinating
5460	well resolved in binoculars, widely scattered in telescopes
5822	easy for binoculars, ample stars in telescopes

STAR		Mag.	Spec.	Name, Comments	Dist.	R.A.	Dec.
ι	Cen	2^m8	A2 V	. . . .	50 ly	13^h20^m6	$-36^\circ71$
J	Cen	4.3	d B3 V	. . . .	600	13 22.6	-60.99
d	Cen	3.9	G8 II	. . . .	400	13 31.0	-39.41
ε	Cen	2.3	B1 IV	. . . .	600	13 39.9	-53.47
Q	Cen	5.0	d B8 V	. . . .	400	13 41.7	-54.56
ν	Cen	3.4	B2 IV	. . . .	600	13 49.5	-41.69
μ	Cen	2.9–3.5	B3 V	. . . .	300	13 49.6	-42.47
ζ	Cen	2.6	B2 IV	. . . .	400	13 55.5	-47.29
φ	Cen	3.8	B2 IV	. . . .	800	13 58.3	-42.10
v^1	Cen	3.9	B3 IV	. . . .	600	13 58.7	-44.80
β	Cen	0.6	B1 III	**Hadar, Agena** . . .	300	14 03.8	-60.37
5 ϑ	Cen	2.1	K0 III	. . . .	50	14 06.7	-36.37
R	Cen	5.3–11.8	M5 II	. . . .	2000	14 16.6	-59.91
η	Cen	2.4	B2 IV	. . . .	300	14 35.5	-42.16
α	Cen	−0.3	d G4 V	**Rigil Kentaurus, Toliman** 4.4	14 39.6	-60.83
b	Cen	4.0	B3 V	. . . .	500	14 42.0	-37.79
α	Cir	3.2	F0 V	. . . .	50	14 42.5	-64.98
κ	Cen	3.1	B2 IV	. . . .	500	14 59.2	-42.10
δ	Cir	4.6	d O9 V	. . . .	2500	15 16.8	-60.94
β	Cir	4.1	A3 V	. . . .	80	15 17.5	-58.80
γ	Cir	4.5	A5 V	. . . .	500	15 23.4	-59.32

BINARY		Mag.	Spec.	PA	Sep.	Vis.
J	Cen	4^m5 6^m2	B3 B3	343°	$60''$	bn
Q	Cen	5.3 6.7	B8 A0	163	5.3	tl
α	Cen	0.0 1.3	G2 K1 '90	215	19.7	Bn
			1995	218	17.3	tl
			2000	222	14.1	tl
			2005	230	10.5	tl
			2010	245	6.8	tl
δ	Cir	5.1 5.7	O9 B1	323	243	op

VARIABLE STAR

μ Cen	irregular
R Cen	Mira type
Period	546 d
Max.	2447950

Comment on α Cen:
second closest star,
11^m Proxima Cen 4.3 ly

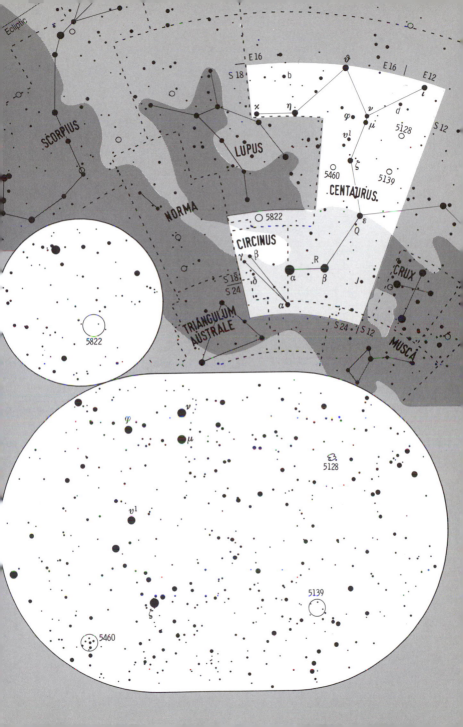

NEBULA	Const.	Mag.	Size	Shape	Type	Vis.	Dist.	R.A.	Dec.
5986	Lup	7^m $8^m_{(5')}$	$6'$	VII	Glob	op	40 000 ly	15^h46^m	$-37°.8$
6067	Nor	6 8	15	r	Open	Ey	6 000	16 13	-54.2
6087	Nor	6 8	15	p	Open	Ey	3 000	16 19	-57.9
6397	Ara	6 9	20	IX	Glob	op	8 000	17 41	-53.7

5986	uniform round nebula, edges can be resolved
6067	bright cluster, very rich in a telescope
6087	nicely resolved in binoculars, low power with telescopes
6397	slightly triangular glow in binoculars, well resolved in telescopes, striking chains of stars at high power

STAR		Mag.	Spec.	Name, Comments	Dist.	R.A.	Dec.
	ι Lup	$3^m.5$	B 3 IV	. . . .	400 ly	$14^h19^m.4$	$-46°.06$
	α Lup	2.3	B 1 III	. . . .	600	14 41.9	-47.39
	β Lup	2.7	B 2 IV	. . . .	500	14 58.5	-43.13
	π Lup	3.9	d B 5 IV	. . . .	400	15 05.1	-47.05
	κ Lup	3.7	d B 9 V	. . . .	200	15 11.9	-48.74
	ζ Lup	3.4	d G 8 III	. . . .	120	15 12.3	-52.10
	μ Lup	4.1	d B 8 V	. . . .	250	15 18.5	-47.88
	δ Lup	3.2	B 2 IV	. . . .	600	15 21.4	-40.65
	φ^1 Lup	3.6	K 5 III	. . . .	200	15 21.8	-36.26
	ϵ Lup	3.4	B 3 IV	. . . .	400	15 22.7	-44.69
	γ Lup	2.8	B 2 IV	. . . .	400	15 35.1	-41.17
d	Lup	4.5	d B 3 IV	. . . .	800	15 35.9	-44.96
	η Lup	3.4	B 2 IV	. . . .	600	16 00.1	-38.40
	γ^2 Nor	4.0	G 8 III	. . . .	120	16 19.8	-50.16
	ϵ Nor	4.4	d B 4 V	. . . .	600	16 27.2	-47.55
	η Ara	3.8	K 5 III	. . . .	200	16 49.8	-59.04
	ζ Ara	3.1	K 4 III	. . . .	120	16 58.6	-55.99
	ϵ^1 Ara	4.1	K 6 III	. . . .	250	16 59.6	-53.16
	β Ara	2.9	K 3 Ib	. . . .	800	17 25.3	-55.53
	γ Ara	3.3	B 1 II	. . . .	1 500	17 25.4	-56.38
	δ Ara	3.6	B 8 V	. . . .	100	17 31.1	-60.68
	α Ara	3.0	B 3 V	. . . .	200	17 31.8	-49.88
	ϑ Ara	3.7	B 2 Ib	. . . .	2 000	18 06.6	-50.09

BINARY		Mag.		Spec.		PA	Sep.	Vis.	Comment on μ Lupi
	π Lup	$4^m.6$	$4^m.7$	B 5	B 5	$63°$	$1''.6$	tl	An interesting
	κ Lup	3.9	5.7	B 9	A 2	144	26.8	Bn	multiple star:
	ζ Lup	3.4	6.7	G 8	F 8	252	71	Bn	double star ($4^m.2$, $7^m.1$)
	μ Lup	5.0	5.1	B 8	B 8	130	1.0	Tl	in binoculars, triple
			7.2		A 0	130	23.6	tl	star ($4^m.3$, $7^m.2$, $7^m.1$)
			7.1		F 5	248	242	Op	in a small telescope,
d	Lup	4.7	6.7	B 3	B 8	10	2.0	tl	quadruple star
	ϵ Nor	4.5	7.5	B 4	B 9	335	22.8	tl	in a large telescope.

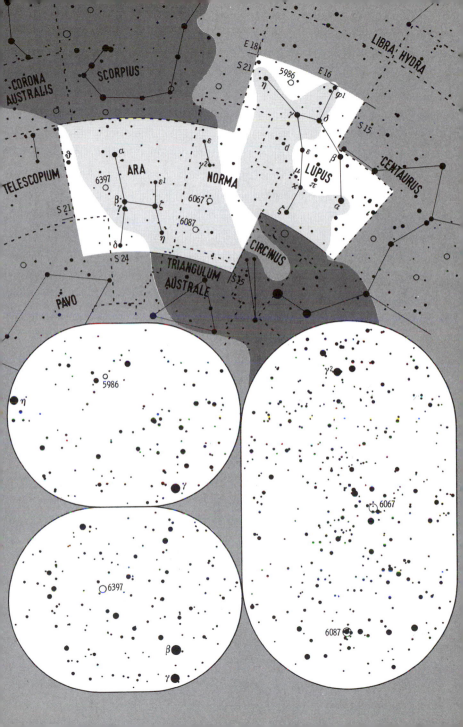

NEBULA	Const.	Mag.		Size	Shape	Type	Vis.	Dist.	R.A.	Dec.
6124	Sco	6^m	$9^m_{(5')}$	$25'$	r	Open	op	2000 ly	16^h26^m	$-40.°7$
6231	Sco	$3\frac{1}{2}$	6	15	p n	Open	ey	4000	16 54	−41.8
6388	Sco	7	7	6	III	Glob	op	40 000	17 36	−44.7
6541	CrA	7	8	8	III	Glob	op	20 000	18 08	−43.7
6723	Sgr	$7\frac{1}{2}$	9	8	VII	Glob	Op	30 000	18 59½	−36.6

6124	resolved in binoculars, background glow from faint stars
6231	one of the brightest clusters, distinct with unaided eye, a few very bright stars in binoculars, some more in telescopes
6388	easily visible as a nebula, not resolved in an amateur telescope
6541	slightly oval and asymmetric, resolved in large telescopes
6723	oval glow in binoculars, partially resolved in large telescopes, faint reflection nebula $30'$ southeast (NGC 6726, 6727)

STAR		Mag.	Spec.	Name, Comments	Dist.	R.A.	Dec.
	μ^1 Sco	$3^m.0$–$3^m.3$	B1 V	} Sep. $5'.8$	600 ly	$16^h51^m.9$	$-38°.05$
	μ^2 Sco	3.6	B2 IV		600	16 52.3	−38.02
	ζ^2 Sco	3.6	K5 III	. . . .	150	16 54.6	−42.36
	η Sco	3.3	F2 IV	. . . .	60	17 12.1	−43.24
34	υ Sco	2.7	B2 III	Lesath	600	17 30.8	−37.30
35	λ Sco	1.6	B2 IV	Shaula	300	17 33.6	−37.10
	ϑ Sco	1.9	F0 II	Sargas	300	17 37.3	−43.00
	κ Sco	2.4	B2 III	. . . .	400	17 42.5	−39.03
	ι^1 Sco	3.0	F2 Ia	. . . .	5000	17 47.6	−40.13
G	Sco	3.2	K2 III	. . . .	150	17 49.9	−37.04
	η Sgr	3.1	d M3 III	. . . .	120	18 17.6	−36.76
	α Tel	3.5	B3 IV	. . . .	500	18 27.0	−45.97
	ζ Tel	4.1	G9 III	. . . .	200	18 28.8	−49.07
	κ CrA	5.2	d B9 V	. . . .	500	18 33.4	−38.72
	ε CrA	4.7–5.0	F1 V	. . . .	90	18 58.7	−37.11
	ζ CrA	4.8	A0 V	. . . .	200	19 03.1	−42.10
	γ CrA	4.2	d F8 V	. . . .	55	19 06.4	−37.06
	δ CrA	4.6	K1 III	. . . .	200	19 08.3	−40.50
	α CrA	4.1	A2 V	. . . .	100	19 09.5	−37.90
	β CrA	4.1	G7 II	. . . .	400	19 10.0	−39.34
	β^1 Sgr	3.9	d B8 V	. . . .	200	19 22.6	−44.46
	α Sgr	4.0	B8 V	. . . .	120	19 23.9	−40.62

BINARY		Mag.	Spec.	PA	Sep.	Vis.
	η Sgr	$3^m.1$ $7^m.8$	M3 G	$105°$	$3''.6$	Tl
	κ CrA	5.7 6.3	B9 A0	5	21.4	Bn
	γ CrA	4.8 5.1	F8 F8 '90	109	1.3	Tl
			2000	55	1.3	Tl
			2010	6	1.4	Tl
	β^1 Sgr	4.0 7.2	B8 A5	77	28.3	tl

VARIABLE STAR

μ^1 Sco β Lyrae type
  Period 1.440269 d
  Min. 2447892.98
ε CrA β Lyrae type
  Period 0.591426 d
  Min. 2447893.00

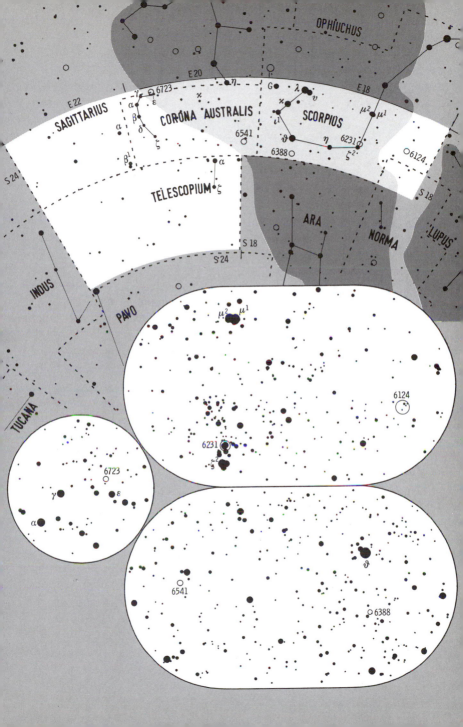

NEBULA	Const.	Mag.	Size	Shape	Type	Vis.	Dist.	R.A.	Dec.
6752	Pav	·5½^m 8$^m_{(5')}$	15'	VI	Glob	Ey	15000 ly	19^{h}11^m	−60°.0

6752   bright globular, well resolved in a telescope, interesting features, remarkable stellar chains, rewarding object

STAR	Mag.	Spec.	Name, Comments	Dist.	R.A.	Dec.
δ Oct	4.3	K2 III	. . . .	200 ly	14^{h}26^m.9	−83°.67
α Aps	3.8	K4 III	. . . .	200	14 47.9	−79.04
γ TrA	2.9	A0 V	. . . .	100	15 18.9	−68.68
ε TrA	4.1	K1 III	. . . .	150	15 36.7	−66.32
β TrA	2.9	F2 V	. . . .	35	15 55.1	−63.43
δ TrA	3.9	G2 II	. . . .	400	16 15.4	−63.69
δ Aps	4.2	d M1 III	. . . .	400	16 20.4	−78.69
γ Aps	3.9	G9 IV	. . . .	70	16 33.5	−78.90
β Aps	4.2	K0 III	. . . .	120	16 43.1	−77.52
α TrA	1.9	K2 III	. . . .	100	16 48.7	−69.03
η Pav	3.6	K2 II	. . . .	300	17 45.7	−64.72
ζ Pav	4.0	K1 III	. . . .	200	18 43.0	−71.43
λ Pav	3.4–4.3	B2 IV	. . . .	1200	18 52.2	−62.19
κ Pav	3.9–4.7	F5 II	. . . .	600	18 56.9	−67.23
ε Pav	4.0	A0 V	. . . .	120	20 00.6	−72.91
δ Pav	3.6	G6 IV	. . . .	19	20 08.7	−66.18
α Pav	1.9	B3 IV	Peacock	250	20 25.6	−56.74
α Ind	3.1	K0 III	. . . .	120	20 37.6	−47.29
β Pav	3.4	A6 III	. . . .	120	20 45.0	−66.20
β Ind	3.7	K1 II	. . . .	400	20 54.8	−58.45
ϑ Ind	4.4	d A5 V	. . . .	100	21 19.9	−53.45
ν Oct	3.8	K0 III	. . . .	90	21 41.5	−77.39
γ Gru	3.0	B8 III	. . . .	250	21 53.9	−37.37
α Gru	1.7	B6 V	Alnair	70	22 08.2	−46.96
α Tuc	2.9	K3 III	. . . .	120	22 18.5	−60.26
π Gru	5.3	d G4 IV	. . . .	200	22 23.0	−45.93
δ¹ Gru	4.0	G6 III	} Sep. 16'.1	150	22 29.3	−43.50
δ² Gru	4.1	M4 III	. . . .	400	22 29.8	−43.75
β Gru	2.1	M4 III	. . . .	150	22 42.7	−46.88
β Oct	4.2	A9 IV	. . . .	100	22 46.1	−81.38
ε Gru	3.5	A2 V	. . . .	80	22 48.6	−51.32
ι Gru	3.9	K0 III	. . . .	150	23 10.4	−45.25
γ Tuc	4.0	F0 III	. . . .	120	23 17.4	−58.24

BINARY	Mag.	Spec.	PA	Sep.	Vis.
δ Aps	4.7 5.3	M5 K4	11°	103"	Op
ϑ Ind	4.5 6.9	A5 A7 '90	270	6.5	tl
		2010	267	6.8	tl
π Gru	5.6 6.6	F2!C	254	261	op

VARIABLE STAR

λ Pav	irregular
κ Pav	Cepheid
Period	9.092 d
Max.	2447897

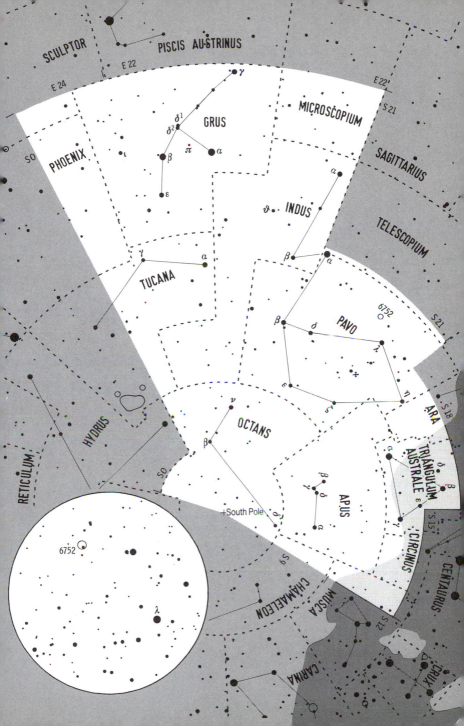

Special Objects

Tables

Special Objects: Extreme values within this catalog (not absolute)

Type, greatest/smallest		Value	Object	Chart
Magnitude	gr.	$-1^{m}_{.}5$ $(-1^{m}_{.}46)$	Sirius, α Canis Majoris	E6
	2nd	-0.7 (-0.72)	Canopus, α Carinae	S3
	3rd	-0.3 (-0.28)	Rigil Kentaurus, α Cen	S15
	4th	0.0 (-0.04)	Arcturus, α Bootis	E15
	5th	0.0 $(0.01-0.04)$	Vega, α Lyrae	N18
	6th	0.1 (0.08)	Capella, α Aurigae	N6
	7th	0.1 (0.12)	Rigel, β Orionis	E4
double star	gr.	0.0 and 1.3	Rigil Kentaurus, α Cen	S15
variable star	gr.	0.4–1.3	Betelgeuse, α Orionis	E5
nebula	gr.	0½	Large Magellanic Cloud	S3
Luminosity	gr.	2×10^{12} suns	Quasar 3C 273	E14
galaxy	gr.	50 000 000 000 suns	Virgo A, M87	E14
diffuse neb.	gr.	20 000 000 suns	Tarantula Nebula, NGC 2070	S3
globular cl.	gr.	800 000 suns	ω Centauri, NGC 5139	S15
open cluster	gr.	100 000 suns	h, χ Persei, NGC 869, 884	N2
planetary neb.	gr.	200 suns	NGC 6818	E22
star	gr.	200 000 suns	β Doradus	S3
	sm.	0.0005 suns	Barnard's Star	E17
Apparent Size	gr.	$480' = 8°$	Large Magellanic Cloud	S3
True Size	gr.	200 000 ly	NGC 4565	E13
diffuse neb.	gr.	1 000 ly	Tarantula Nebula, NGC 2070	S3
globular cl.	gr.	150 ly	M53, NGC 5024	E13
open cluster	gr.	60 ly	h, χ Persei, NGC 869, 884	N2
planetary neb.	gr.	4 ly	Little Dumbbell, M76	N0
nebula	sm.	0.1 ly	NGC 6572	E19
double star	gr.	6 ly	34 φ Cassiopeiae	N2
	sm.	2 000 000 000 km	Alula Australis, ξ UMa	N12
star	gr.	1 500 000 000 km	Y Canum Venaticorum	N12
	sm.	20 000 km	o^2 Eridani companion	E2
Distance	gr.	2 000 000 000 ly	Quasar 3C 273	E14
	2nd	60 000 000 ly	Fornax (Galaxy) Cluster	S0
star	gr.	10 000 ly	34 φ Cassiopeiae	N2
	sm.	4.4 ly	Rigil Kentaurus, α Cen	S15
bluest star		spectral type O5	ζ Puppis	S6
reddest star		spectral type C6	R Leporis	E4
gr. color contrast		spectr. t. M1, B3	Antares, α Scorpii	E18
gr. rotation 1990–2000		$147°$ in 10 years	Alula Australis, ξ UMa	N12
gr. rotation 2000–2010		$223°$ in 10 years	Porrima, γ Virginis	E12
gr. change in separation		$7''$ in 10 years	Rigil Kentaurus, α Cen	S15
gr. proper motion		$10''$ per year	Barnard's Star	E17
gr. period		27 years	ε Aurigae	N6
sm. period		2 minutes	Suhail Al Muhlif, γ Vel	S6
gr. amplitude		$10^{m}_{.}9$ $(3^{m}_{.}3-14^{m}_{.}2)$	χ Cygni	N18

Sidereal Time, Meteor Showers

Standard Time						Right Ascension in the						
18–19^h	20–21^h	22–23^h	0–1^h	2–3^h	4–5^h	East			Meridian			West
Dec.	Nov.	Oct.	Sept.	Aug.	July	6^h	4^h	2^h	0^h	22^h	20^h	18^h
Jan.	Dec.	Nov.	Oct.	Sept.	Aug.	8	6	4	**2**	0	22	20
Feb.	Jan.	Dec.	Nov.	Oct.	Sept.	10	8	6	**4**	2	0	22
Mar.	Feb.	Jan.	Dec.	Nov.	Oct.	12	10	8	**6**	4	2	0
Apr.	Mar.	Feb.	Jan.	Dec.	Nov.	14	12	10	**8**	6	4	2
May	Apr.	Mar.	Feb.	Jan.	Dec.	16	14	12	**10**	8	6	4
June	May	Apr.	Mar.	Feb.	Jan.	18	16	14	**12**	10	8	6
July	June	May	Apr.	Mar.	Feb.	20	18	16	**14**	12	10	8
Aug.	July	June	May	Apr.	Mar.	22	20	18	**16**	14	12	10
Sept.	Aug.	July	June	May	Apr.	0	22	20	**18**	16	14	12
Oct.	Sept.	Aug.	July	June	May	2	0	22	**20**	18	16	14
Nov.	Oct.	Sept.	Aug.	July	June	4	2	0	**22**	20	18	16
19–20^h	21–22^h	23–24^h	1–2^h	3–4^h	5–6^h	**Sidereal**						
	Daylight Saving Time							**Time**				

Sidereal Time$(^h)$ = (J.D. − 2447790.66) / 15.2184 + UT + East.Long. / $15^°$

The table above makes it easy to estimate the sidereal time. Find the relevant time and look down the column to the current month. Then move horizontally to the right. The bold number is the sidereal time, which is the right ascension on the meridian. To the left and right are right-ascension hours of the eastern and western celestial hemisphere. Much higher accuracy (to about one second) can be achieved by using the formula above (for J.D. − see pp. 122, 123).
Example for Sydney ($151^°13'$ east) on February 10, 1990, 6^h12^m daylight time (11^h ahead of UT): in column 5–6^h one finds Feb. in the eighth row; the right-hand side shows $\approx 14^h$ sidereal time. Accurate calculation: sidereal time = (2447932.30 − 2447790.66) / 15.2184 + $6\frac{12}{60}$ − 11 + $151\frac{13}{60}$ / 15 = $14^h.588$ = $14^h35^m.3$.

Meteor Shower	Start	Max.	End	Time	Rate	Radiant		Speed	Source Comet
Quadrantids	Jan 2	Jan 3	Jan 4	0–7^h	40/h	15^h20^m	$+50^°$	$45\frac{km}{s}$	plan.?
Lyrids	Apr 15	Apr 22	Apr 24	21–4	10	18 10	+35	50	1861 I
η Aquarids	May 1	May 5	May 10	3–4	15	22 30	0	65	Halley
δ Aquarids	Jul 24	Jul 31	Aug 10	0–3	15	23 00	−15	30	ecliptic
Perseids	Jul 28	Aug 11	Aug 20	21–4	80	3 00	+58	60	1862 III
Orionids	Oct 15	Oct 20	Oct 25	23–6	15	6 20	+15	65	Halley
Taurids	Oct 20	Nov 11	Nov 30	19–6	10	4 00	+20	30	Encke?
Leonids	Nov 15	Nov 17	Nov 19	1–6	10	10 10	+20	70	1866 I
Geminids	Dec 8	Dec 13	Dec 15	19–7	50	7 30	+30	35	m. planet
Ursids	Dec 20	Dec 22	Dec 23	18–7	10	14 30	+75	35	Tuttle?

Time: period of visibility for northern-hemisphere observers
Rate: meteor frequency at maximum, radiant at zenith (zenith hourly rate)

Summary 1990–1999

Year 19	90		91		92		93		94		95		96		97		98		99	
Moon	Nw	Fl	Nw	Fl	Nw	Fl	Nw	Fl	Nw	Fl	Nw	Fl	Nw	Fl	Nw	Fl	Nw	Fl	Nw	Fl
Jan.	<u>26</u>	11	<u>15</u>	<u>30</u>	<u>4</u>	19	22	8	11	27	$\frac{1}{30}$	16	20	5	9	23	28	12	17	$\frac{2}{31}$
Feb.	25	<u>9</u>	14	28	3	18	21	6	10	26	—	15	18	4	7	22	<u>26</u>	11	<u>16</u>	—
Mar.	26	11	16	30	4	18	23	8	12	27	$\frac{1}{31}$	17	19	5	<u>9</u>	24	28	<u>13</u>	17	$\frac{2}{31}$
Apr.	25	10	14	28	3	17	21	6	11	25	<u>29</u>	<u>15</u>	<u>17</u>	<u>4</u>	7	22	26	11	16	30
May	24	9	14	28	2	16	<u>21</u>	6	<u>10</u>	<u>25</u>	29	14	17	3	6	22	25	11	15	30
June	22	8	12	27	$\frac{1}{30}$	<u>15</u>	20	<u>4</u>	9	23	28	13	16	1	5	20	24	10	13	28
July	<u>22</u>	8	<u>11</u>	26	29	14	19	3	8	22	27	12	15	$\frac{1}{30}$	4	20	23	9	13	<u>28</u>
Aug.	20	<u>6</u>	10	25	28	13	17	2	7	21	26	10	14	28	3	18	<u>22</u>	8	<u>11</u>	26
Sept.	19	5	8	23	26	12	16	$\frac{1}{30}$	5	19	24	9	12	<u>27</u>	<u>1</u>	<u>16</u>	20	<u>6</u>	9	25
Oct.	18	4	7	23	25	11	15	30	5	19	<u>24</u>	<u>8</u>	<u>12</u>	26	$\frac{1}{31}$	16	20	5	9	24
Nov.	17	2	6	<u>21</u>	24	10	<u>13</u>	29	<u>3</u>	18	22	7	11	25	30	14	19	4	8	23
Dec.	17	$\frac{2}{31}$	6	<u>21</u>	<u>24</u>	9	13	28	2	18	22	7	10	24	29	14	18	3	7	22

Year 19	90	91	92	93	94	95	96	97	98	99
Mercury E.	—	—	Mar 9	Feb 21	Feb 4	Jan 19	Jan 2	—	—	Mar 3
West	Feb 1	Jan 14	Apr 23	Apr 5	Mar 19	Mar 1	Feb 11	Jan 24	Jan 6	Apr 16
East	Apr 13	Mar 27	Jul 6	Jun 17	May 30	May 12	Apr 23	Apr 6	Mar 20	Jun 28
West	May 31	May 12	Aug 21	Aug 4	Jul 17	Jun 29	Jun 10	May 22	May 4	Aug 14
East	Aug 11	Jul 25	Oct 31	Oct 14	Sep 26	Sep 9	Aug 21	Aug 4	Jul 17	Oct 24
West	Sep 24	Sep 7	Dec 9	Nov 22	Nov 6	Oct 20	Oct 3	Sep 16	Aug 31	Dec 3
East	Dec 6	Nov 19	—	—	—	—	Dec 15	Nov 28	Nov 11	—
West	—	Dec 27	—	—	—	—	—	—	Dec 20	—
Venus East	—	Jun 13	—	Jan 19	Aug 24	—	Apr 1	Nov 6	—	Jun 11
West	Mar 30	Nov 2	—	Jun 10	—	Jan 13	Aug 20	—	Mar 27	Oct 30
Mars	Nov 27	—	—	Jan 7	—	Feb 12	—	Mar 17	—	Apr 24
Const.	Tau	—	—	Gem	—	Leo	—	Vir	—	Vir
Jupiter	—	Jan 29	Feb 29	Mar 30	Apr 30	Jun 1	Jul 4	Aug 9	Sep 16	Oct 23
Const.	—	Cnc	Leo	Vir	Lib	Oph	Sgr	Cap	Aqr	Ari
Saturn	Jul 14	Jul 27	Aug 7	Aug 19	Sep 1	Sep 14	Sep 26	Oct 10	Oct 23	Nov 6
Const.	Sgr	Cap	Cap	Aqr	Aqr	Aqr	Psc	Psc	Psc	Ari

Julian Date	244....	244....	244....	244....	244....	244....	245....	245....	245....	245....
Jan.	7892	8257	8622	8988	9353	9718	0083	0449	0814	1179
Feb.	7923	8288	8653	9019	9384	9749	0114	0480	0845	1210
Mar.	7951	8316	8682	9047	9412	9777	0143	0508	0873	1238
Apr.	7982	8347	8713	9078	9443	9808	0174	0539	0904	1269
May	8012	8377	8743	9108	9473	9838	0204	0569	0934	1299
June	8043	8408	8774	9139	9504	9869	0235	0600	0965	1330
July	8073	8438	8804	9169	9534	9899	0265	0630	0995	1360
Aug.	8104	8469	8835	9200	9565	9930	0296	0661	1026	1391
Sept.	8135	8500	8866	9231	9596	9961	0327	0692	1057	1422
Oct.	8165	8530	8896	9261	9626	9991	0357	0722	1087	1452
Nov.	8196	8561	8927	9292	9657	'0022	0388	0753	1118	1483
Dec.	8226	8591	8957	9322	9687	'0052	0418	0783	1148	1513

New Moon, Full Moon: solar and lunar eclipses are underscored
Mercury, Venus: greatest eastern / western elongation (evening / morning star)
Mars, Jupiter, Saturn: date of opposition (best visibility) and position

Year 20	00 Nw Fl	01 Nw Fl	02 Nw Fl	03 Nw Fl	04 Nw Fl	05 Nw Fl	06 Nw Fl	07 Nw Fl	08 Nw Fl	09 Nw Fl	10 Nw Fl
Moon											
Jan.	6 21	24 9	13 28	2 18	21 7	10 25	29 14	19 3	8 22	26 11	15 30
Feb.	5 19	23 8	12 27	1 16	20 6	8 24	28 13	17 2	7 21	25 9	14 28
Mar.	6 20	25 9	14 28	3 18	20 6	10 25	29 14	19 3	7 21	26 11	15 30
Apr.	4 18	23 8	12 27	1 16	19 5	8 24	27 13	17 2	6 20	25 9	14 28
May	4 18	23 7	12 26	3¹ 16	19 4	8 23	27 13	16 2	5 20	24 9	14 27
June	2 16	21 6	10 24	29 14	17 3	6 22	25 11	15 30	3 18	22 7	12 26
July	3¹ 16	20 5	10 24	29 13	17 3¹	6 21	25 11	14 30	3 18	22 7	11 26
Aug.	29 15	19 4	8 22	27 12	16 30	5 19	23 9	12 28	30¹ 16	20 6	10 24
Sept.	27 13	17 2	7 21	26 10	14 28	3 18	22 7	11 26	29 15	18 4	7 23
Oct.	27 13	16 2	6 21	25 10	14 28	3 17	22 7	11 26	28 14	18 4	7 23
Nov.	25 11	15 30	4 20	23 9	12 26	2 16	20 5	9 24	27 13	16 2	6 21
Dec.	25 11	14 30	4 19	23 8	12 26	3¹ 15	20 5	9 24	27 12	16 3²	5 21

	00	01	02	03	04	05	06	07	08	09	10
Merc. E.	Feb 15	Jan 28	Jan 11	-	-	Mar 12	Feb 24	Feb 7	Jan 22	Jan 4	-
West	Mar 28	Mar 11	Feb 21	Feb 4	Jan 17	Apr 26	Apr 8	Mar 22	Mar 3	Feb 13	Jan 27
East	Jun 9	May 22	May 4	Apr 16	Mar 29	Jul 9	Jun 20	Jun 2	May 14	Apr 26	Apr 8
West	Jul 27	Jul 9	Jun 21	Jun 3	May 14	Aug 23	Aug 7	Jul 20	Jul 1	Jun 13	May 26
East	Oct 6	Sep 18	Sep 1	Aug 14	Jul 27	Nov 3	Oct 17	Sep 29	Sep 11	Aug 24	Aug 7
West	Nov 15	Oct 29	Oct 13	Sep 27	Sep 9	Dec 12	Nov 25	Nov 8	Oct 22	Oct 6	Sep 19
East	-	-	Dec 26	Dec 9	Nov 21	-	-	-	-	Dec 18	Dec 1
West	-	-	-	-	Dec 29	-	-	-	-	-	-
Venus E.	-	Jan 17	Aug 22	-	Mar 29	Nov 3	-	Jun 9	-	Jan 14	Aug 20
West	-	Jun 8	-	Jan 11	Aug 17	-	Mar 25	Oct 28	-	Jun 5	-
Mars	-	Jun 13	-	Aug 28	-	Nov 7	-	Dec 24	-	-	Jan 29
Const.	-	Oph	-	Aqr	-	Ari	-	Gem	-	-	Cnc
Jupiter	Nov 28	-	Jan 1	Feb 2	Mar 4	Apr 3	May 4	Jun 6	Jul 9	Aug 14	Sep 21
Const.	Tau	-	Gem	Cnc	Leo	Vir	Lib	Oph	Sgr	Cap	Psc
Saturn	Nov 19	Dec 3	Dec 17	Dec 31	-	Jan 13	Jan 27	Feb 10	Feb 24	Mar 8	Mar 22
Const.	Tau	Tau	Tau	Gem	-	Gem	Cnc	Leo	Leo	Leo	Vir
Julian D.	245....	245....	245....	245....	245....	245....	245....	245....	245....	245....	245....
Jan.	1544	1910	2275	2640	3005	3371	3736	4101	4466	4832	5197
Feb.	1575	1941	2306	2671	3036	3402	3767	4132	4497	4863	5228
Mar.	1604	1969	2334	2699	3065	3430	3795	4160	4526	4891	5256
Apr.	1635	2000	2365	2730	3096	3461	3826	4191	4557	4922	5287
May	1665	2030	2395	2760	3126	3491	3856	4221	4587	4952	5317
June	1696	2061	2426	2791	3157	3522	3887	4252	4618	4983	5348
July	1726	2091	2456	2821	3187	3552	3917	4282	4648	5013	5378
Aug.	1757	2122	2487	2852	3218	3583	3948	4313	4679	5044	5409
Sept.	1788	2153	2518	2883	3249	3614	3979	4344	4710	5075	5440
Oct.	1818	2183	2548	2913	3279	3644	4009	4374	4740	5105	5470
Nov.	1849	2214	2579	2944	3310	3675	4040	4405	4771	5136	5501
Dec.	1879	2244	2609	2974	3340	3705	4070	4435	4801	5166	5531

Julian Date = entry in table + day of month + $(UT - 12^h) / 24^h$
Example for February 9, 1990, 19^h12^m Universal Time :
J.D. = 2440000 + 7923 + 9 + $(19\tfrac{12}{60} - 12) / 24$ = 2 447 932.300

Nebula Numbers

M	Chart	M	Chart
M1	E3	M56	N18
M2	E24	M57	N18
M3	E15	M58	E14
M4	E18	M59	E14
M5	E15	M60	E14
M6	E18	M61	E14
M7	E18	M62	E18
M8	E20	M63	N12
M9	E17	M64	E13
M10	E17	M65	E11
M11	E19	M66	E11
M12	E17	M67	E9
M13	N14	M68	E12
M14	E17	M69	E20
M15	E23	M70	E20
M16	E20	M71	E21
M17	E20	M72	E24
M18	E20	M73	E24
M19	E18	M74	E1
M20	E20	M75	E22
M21	E20	M76	N0
M22	E20	M77	E0
M23	E20	M78	E5
M24	E20	M79	E4
M25	E20	M80	E18
M26	E19	M81	N8
M27	E21	M82	N8
M28	E20	M83	E16
M29	N20	M84	E14
M30	E22	M85	E14
M31	N0	M86	E14
M32	N0	M87	E14
M33	N0	M88	E14
M34	N4	M89	E14
M35	E7	M90	E14
M36	N6	M91	E14
M37	N6	M92	N14
M38	N6	M93	E6
M39	N24	M94	N12
M40	N10	M95	E11
M41	E6	M96	E11
M42	E4	M97	N10
M43	E4	M98	E14
M44	E9	M99	E14
M45	E3	M100	E14
M46	E8	M101	N10
M47	E8	M102	N16
M48	E10	M103	N2
M49	E14	M104	E12
M50	E8	M105	E11
M51	N12	M106	N12
M52	N22	M107	E17
M53	E13	M108	N10
M54	E20	M109	N10
M55	E22	M110	N0

NGC	Chart	NGC	Chart	NGC	Chart	NGC	Chart	NGC	Chart
55	S0	2068	E5	3242	E10	4736	N12	6543	N16
104	S0	2070	S3	3293	S9	4755	S12	6572	E19
205	N0	2099	N6	3351	E11	4762	E14	6611	E20
221	N0	2129	E7	3368	E11	4826	E13	6613	E20
224	N0	2168	E7	3372	S9	5024	E13	6618	E20
247	E0	2175	E7	3379	E11	5055	N12	6626	E20
253	E0	2237	E9	3384	E11	5128	S15	6633	E19
281	N2	2244	E9	3532	S9	5139	S15	6637	E20
288	E0	2261	E7	3556	N10	5194	N12	6656	E20
292	S0	2264	E7	3587	N10	5195	N12	6681	E20
362	S0	2281	N6	3623	E11	5236	E16	6694	E19
457	N2	2287	E6	3627	E11	5272	E15	6705	E19
559	N2	2301	E9	3628	E11	5457	N10	6712	E19
581	N2	2323	E8	3766	S12	5460	S15	6715	E20
598	N0	2324	E9	3992	N10	5746	E15	6720	N18
628	E1	2359	E1	4192	E14	5822	S15	6723	S21
650	N0	2360	E8	4216	E14	5866	N16	6752	S24
654	N2	2362	E6	4244	N12	5904	E15	6779	N18
663	N2	2392	E7	4254	E14	5907	N16	6809	E22
752	N0	2403	N8	4258	N12	5986	S18	6818	E22
869	N2	2422	E8	4303	E14	6067	S18	6822	E22
884	N2	2423	E8	4321	E14	6087	S18	6826	N18
891	N0	2437	E8	4361	E12	6093	E18	6838	E21
1023	N4	2438	E8	4374	E14	6121	E18	6853	E21
1039	N4	2447	E6	4382	E14	6124	S21	6864	E22
1068	E0	2451	S6	4406	E14	6171	E17	6913	N20
1245	N4	2477	S6	4449	N12	6205	N14	6939	N22
1291	S0	2516	S3	4472	E14	6210	E19	6940	N20
1316	S0	2539	E8	4486	E14	6218	E17	6946	N22
1360	E2	2546	S6	4490	N12	6231	S21	6960	N20
1365	S0	2547	S6	4494	E13	6254	E17	6981	E24
1491	N4	2548	E10	4501	E14	6266	E18	6992	N20
1528	N4	2632	E9	4526	E14	6273	E18	6994	E24
1535	E2	2682	E9	4548	E14	6333	E17	7000	N20
1647	E3	2683	N8	4552	E14	6341	N14	7009	E24
1788	E5	2808	S9	4559	E13	6369	E18	7027	N20
1851	S3	2841	N8	4565	E13	6388	S21	7078	E23
1904	E4	2903	E11	4569	E14	6397	S18	7089	E24
1912	N6	2976	N8	4579	E14	6402	E17	7092	N24
1931	N6	3031	N8	4590	E12	6405	E18	7099	E22
1952	E3	3034	N8	4594	E12	6475	E18	7209	N24
1960	N6	3077	N8	4621	E14	6494	E20	7243	N24
1973	E4	3114	S9	4631	E13	6503	N16	7293	E24
1976	E4	3115	E10	4649	E14	6514	E20	7331	E23
1981	E4	3132	S6	4656	E13	6523	E20	7654	N22
1982	E4	3184	N10	4697	E12	6531	E20	7662	N24
2024	E5	3201	S6	4725	E13	6541	S21	7789	N22

IC	Chart	Named object	Identification	Chart
IC 1396	N22	η Carinae Nebula	= NGC 3372	S9
IC 2391	S6	o Velorum Cluster	= IC 2391	S6
IC 2602	S9	ω Centauri	= NGC 5139	S15
IC 4665	E17	47 Tucanae	= NGC 104	S0
IC 4725	E20	Centaurus A	= NGC 5128	S15
IC 4756	E19	Fornax A	= NGC 1316	S0
IC 5067	N20	Virgo A	= M87	E14

Nebula Names

Nebula Name	NGC	Messier	Chart	Const.	Type	Vis.
Andromeda Galaxy	224	M31	N0	And	Galx	ey
Barnard's Galaxy	6822		E22	Sgr	Galx	Bn
Black Eye Galaxy	4826	M64	E13	Com	Galx	Op
Blinking Planetary	6826		N18	Cyg	Plan	Op
Blue Snowball	7662		N24	And	Plan	Op
Butterfly Cluster	6405	M6	E18	Sco	Open	ey
Christmas Tree (Cluster)	2264		E7	Mon	Open	ey
Coalsack			S12	Cru	Dark N.	ey
Coma (Star) Cluster			E13	Com	Open	ey
Crab Nebula	1952	M1	E3	Tau	Diff	bn
Double Cluster, h and χ Persei	869, 884		N2	Per	Open	ey
Dumbbell Nebula	6853	M27	E21	Vul	Plan	Op
Eagle Nebula	6611	M16	E20	Ser	Diff	op
Eskimo Nebula	2392		E7	Gem	Plan	bn
Fornax (Galaxy) Cluster			S0	For	(Galx)	Bn
Ghost of Jupiter	3242		E10	Hya	Plan	Op
Helix Nebula	7293		E24	Aqr	Plan	op
Hercules Cluster	6205	M13	N14	Her	Glob	Ey
Hubble's Variable Nebula	2261		E7	Mon	Diff	Bn
Hyades			E3	Tau	Open	ey
Jewel Box, κ Crucis (Cluster)	4755		S12	Cru	Open	ey
Lagoon Nebula	6523	M8	E20	Sgr	Diff	ey
Large Magellanic Cloud		LMC	S3	Dor	Galx	ey
Little Dumbbell (Nebula)	650	M76	N0	Per	Plan	tl
Makarian's (Galaxy) Chain		M86–M88	E14	Com	(Galx)	tl
North America Nebula	7000		N20	Cyg	Diff	Ey
Omega Nebula, Swan Nebula	6618	M17	E20	Sgr	Diff	op
Orion Nebula	1976	M42	E4	Ori	Diff	ey
Owl Nebula	3587	M97	N10	UMa	Plan	tl
Pelican Nebula	IC 5067		N20	Cyg	Diff	bn
Pinwheel Galaxy	5457	M101	N10	UMa	Galx	bn
Pleiades, Seven Sisters		M45	E3	Tau	Open	ey
Praesepe, Beehive (Cluster)	2632	M44	E9	Cnc	Open	ey
Quasi–stellar object 3C 273			E14	Vir	Quasar	Tl
Ring Nebula	6720	M57	N18	Lyr	Plan	Op
Rosette Nebula	2237		E9	Mon	Diff	bn
Saturn Nebula	7009		E24	Aqr	Plan	Op
Sculptor Galaxy	253		E0	Scl	Galx	op
Small Magellanic Cloud	292	SMC	S0	Tuc	Galx	ey
Sombrero Galaxy	4594	M104	E12	Vir	Galx	Op
Southern Pleiades	IC 2602		S9	Car	Open	ey
Spindle Galaxy	3115		E10	Sex	Galx	bn
Tarantula Nebula	2070		S3	Dor	Diff	ey
Triangulum Galaxy	598	M33	N0	Tri	Galx	op
Trifid Nebula	6514	M20	E20	Sgr	Diff	Op
Veil Nebula ⎧Filamentary Nebula	6960		N20	Cyg	Diff	tl
Cirrus N. ⎨Network Nebula	6992		N20	Cyg	Diff	Bn
Virgo (Galaxy) Cluster			E14	Vir	(Galx)	Bn
Whirlpool Galaxy	5194	M51	N12	CVn	Galx	bn

Star Names

Star Name	Designat.		Chart	Mag.
Acamar	ϑ	Eri	S0	3^{m}0
Achernar	α	Eri	S0	0.5
Acrab	β	Sco	E18	2.5
Acrux	α	Cru	S12	0.8
Acubens	α	Cnc	E9	4.3
Adhara	ε	CMa	E6	1.5
Agena	β	Cen	S15	0.6
Alamak	γ	And	N0	2.2
Albireo	β	Cyg	N18	2.9
Alchiba	α	Crv	E12	4.0
Alcor	80	UMa	N10	4.0
Alcyone	η	Tau	E3	2.8
Aldebaran	α	Tau	E3	0.9
Alderamin	α	Cep	N22	2.4
Aldhafera	ζ	Leo	E11	3.4
Alfirk	β	Cep	N22	3.2
Algenib	γ	Peg	E1	2.8
Algieba	γ	Leo	E11	2.1
Algiedi	α	Cap	E22	3.1
Algol	β	Per	N4	2–3
Algorab	δ	Crv	E12	3.0
Alhena	γ	Gem	E7	1.9
Alioth	ε	UMa	N10	1.8
Alkaid	η	UMa	N10	1.9
Alkalurops	μ	Boo	N14	4.2
Alkes	α	Crt	E12	4.1
Alnair	α	Gru	S24	1.7
Alnasl	γ	Sgr	E20	3.0
Alnilam	ε	Ori	E5	1.7
Alnitak	ζ	Ori	E5	1.8
Alphard	α	Hya	E10	2.0
Alphekka	α	CrB	E15	2.3
Alpheratz	α	And	N0	2.0
Alshain	β	Aql	E21	3.7
Altair	α	Aql	E21	0.8
Altais	δ	Dra	N16	3.1
Altarf	β	Cnc	E9	3.5
Alterf	λ	Leo	E11	4.3
Aludra	η	CMa	E6	2.4
Alula Australis	ξ	UMa	N12	3.8
Alula Borealis	ν	UMa	N12	3.5
Alya	ϑ	Ser	E19	4.0
Ankaa	α	Phe	S0	2.4
Antares	α	Sco	E18	1–2
Arcturus	α	Boo	E15	0.0
Arneb	α	Lep	E4	2.6
Asellus Australis	δ	Cnc	E9	3.9
Asellus Borealis	γ	Cnc	E9	4.7
Aspidiske	ξ	Pup	E6	3^{m}2
Atair	α	Aql	E21	0.8
Atik	o	Per	N4	3.8
Atlas	27	Tau	E3	3.6
Avior	ε	Car	S3	1.9
Baham	ϑ	Peg	E23	3.5
Barnard's Star			E17	9.5
Baten Kaitos	ζ	Cet	E0	3.7
Bellatrix	γ	Ori	E5	1.6
Benetnasch	η	UMa	N10	1.9
Betelgeuse	α	Ori	E5	0–1
Canopus	α	Car	S3	−0.7
Capella	α	Aur	N6	0.1
Castor	α	Gem	E7	1.6
Cebalrai	β	Oph	E17	2.8
Ceginus	γ	Boo	N14	3.0
Chaph	β	Cas	N2	2.3
Cor Caroli	α	CVn	N12	2.8
Coxa	ϑ	Leo	E11	3.3
Cursa	β	Eri	E2	2.8
Deneb	α	Cyg	N20	1.3
Deneb Algedi	δ	Cap	E22	3
Deneb Kaitos	β	Cet	E0	2.0
Denebola	β	Leo	E11	2.1
Diadem	α	Com	E13	4.3
Diphda	β	Cet	E0	2.0
Dubhe	α	UMa	N10	1.8
Edasich	ι	Dra	N16	3.3
Electra	17	Tau	E3	3.7
Elmuthalleth	α	Tri	N0	3.4
Elnath	β	Tau	E3	1.7
Enif	ε	Peg	E23	2.4
Errai	γ	Cep	N22	3.2
Ettanin	γ	Dra	N16	2.2
Fomalhaut	α	PsA	E22	1.2
Gacrux	γ	Cru	S12	1.6
Gemma	α	CrB	E15	2.3
Giauzar	λ	Dra	N16	3.8
Gienah	γ	Crv	E12	2.6
Gomeisa	β	CMi	E9	2.9
Grumium	ξ	Dra	N16	3.8
Hadar	β	Cen	S15	0.6
Hamal	α	Ari	E1	2.0
Homam	ζ	Peg	E23	3.4
Izar	ε	Boo	E15	2.4
Kaus Australis	ε	Sgr	E20	1.8
Kaus Borealis	λ	Sgr	E20	2.8
Kaus Media	δ	Sgr	E20	2.7

Star Names

Star Name	Designat.	Chart	Mag.
Kitalphar . . α	Equ	E23	3.9
Kochab . . . β	UMi	NP	2.1
La Superba . γ	CVn	N12	6
Lesath . . . υ	Sco	S21	2.7
Maia 20	Tau	E3	3.9
Marfik . . . λ	Oph	E17	3.8
Markab . . . α	Peg	E23	2.5
Matar . . . η	Peg	E23	2.9
Mebsuta . . ε	Gem	E7	3.0
Megrez . . . δ	UMa	N10	3.3
Mekbuda . . ζ	Gem	E7	4
Menkalinan . β	Aur	N6	1.9
Menkar . . . α	Cet	E0	2.5
Menkib . . ξ	Per	N4	4.0
Merak . . . β	UMa	N10	2.4
Merope . . 23	Tau	E3	4.2
Mesarthim . γ	Ari	E1	3.9
Miaplacidus . β	Car	S9	1.7
Mimosa . . . β	Cru	S12	1.3
Mintaka . . δ	Ori	E5	2.2
Mira . . . . o	Cet	E0	2–10
Mirach . . . β	And	N0	2.1
Mirphak . . α	Per	N4	1.8
Mirzam . . . β	CMa	E6	2.0
Mizar . . . ζ	UMa	N10	2.1
Muphrid . . η	Boo	E15	2.7
Nath . . . . β	Tau	E3	1.7
Nekkar . . . β	Boo	N14	3.5
Nihal . . . . β	Lep	E4	2.8
North Star . α	UMi	NP	2.0
Nunki . . . . σ	Sgr	E20	2.0
Nusakan . . β	CrB	E15	3.7
Peacock . . . α	Pav	S24	1.9
Phact . . . . α	Col	E2	2.6
Phad . . . . γ	UMa	N10	2.4
Phegda . . . γ	UMa	N10	2.4
Pherkad . . . γ	UMi	NP	3.1
Phurud . . . ζ	CMa	E6	3.0
Piazzi's Flying St. 61	Cyg	N24	4.8
Pleione . . 28	Tau	E3	5–6
Polaris . . . α	UMi	NP	2.0
Pollux . . . β	Gem	E7	1.1
Porrima . . . γ	Vir	E12	2.8
Procyon . . . α	CMi	E9	0.4
Pulcherrima . ε	Boo	E15	2.4
Rasalgethi . α	Her	E19	3–4
Rasalhague . α	Oph	E17	2.1
Rastaben . . β	Dra	N16	2.8

Star Name	Designat.	Chart	Mag.
Regulus . . . α	Leo	E11	1.4
Rigel . . . . β	Ori	E4	0.1
Rigil Kentaurus α	Cen	S15	−0.3
Ruchbah . . δ	Cas	N2	2.7
Ruticulus . . β	Her	E19	2.8
Sabik . . . . η	Oph	E17	2.4
Sadachbia . . γ	Aqr	E24	3.8
Sadalbari . . μ	Peg	E23	3.5
Sadalmelik . α	Aqr	E24	3.0
Sadalsuud . . β	Aqr	E24	2.9
Sadr . . . . γ	Cyg	N20	2.2
Saiph . . . . κ	Ori	E4	2.1
Sargas . . . ϑ	Sco	S21	1.9
Scheat . . . β	Peg	E23	2–3
Schedir . . . α	Cas	N2	2.2
Shaula . . . λ	Sco	S21	1.6
Sheliak . . . β	Lyr	N18	3–4
Sheratan . . β	Ari	E1	2.6
Sirius . . . . α	CMa	E6	−1.5
Sirrah . . . α	And	N0	2.0
Spica . . . . α	Vir	E16	1.0
Suhail Al Muhlif γ	Vel	S6	2
Suhail Al Wazn λ	Vel	S6	2.2
Sulaphat . . γ	Lyr	N18	3.2
Talitha . . . ι	UMa	N8	3.1
Tania Australis μ	UMa	N10	3.1
Tania Borealis λ	UMa	N10	3.5
Tarazed . . . γ	Aql	E21	2.7
Taygeta . . . 19	Tau	E3	4.3
Tejat Posterior μ	Gem	E7	2.9
Tejat Prior . η	Gem	E7	3–4
The Double Double ε	Lyr	N18	3.9
Thuban . . . α	Dra	N16	3.7
Toliman . . . α	Cen	S15	−0.3
Trapezium . . ϑ^1	Ori	E4	4.7
Unukalhai . . α	Ser	E16	2.7
Vega . . . . α	Lyr	N18	0.0
Vindemiatrix . ε	Vir	E16	2.8
Wasat . . . . δ	Gem	E7	3.5
Wezen . . . . δ	CMa	E6	1.8
Yed Posterior ε	Oph	E17	3.2
Yed Prior . . δ	Oph	E17	2.7
Zaniah . . . η	Vir	E12	3.9
Zaurak . . . γ	Eri	E2	3.0
Zavijava . . β	Vir	E12	3.6
Zosma . . . δ	Leo	E11	2.6
Zubenelgenubi α	Lib	E16	2.6
Zubeneschemali β	Lib	E16	2.6

Abbr.	Constellation	Genitive	Meaning	Chart	Neb.	St.
And	Andromeda	Andromedae	(myth. name)	N0 (N24)	6	16
Ant	Antlia	Antliae	Air Pump	E10	-	1
Aps	Apus	Apodis	Bird of Paradise	S24	-	4
Aqr	Aquarius	Aquarii	Water-bearer	E24	5	19
Aql	Aquila	Aquilae	Eagle	E21	-	15
Ara	Ara	Arae	Altar	S18	1	8
Ari	Aries	Arietis	Ram	E1	-	8
Aur	Auriga	Aurigae	Charioteer	N6	5	14
Boo	Boötes	Boötis	Herdsman	E15 (N14)	-	18
Cae	Caelum	Caeli	Chisel	S3	-	-
Cam	Camelopardalis	Camelopadalis	Giraffe	N2 (NP)	1	6
Cnc	Cancer	Cancri ⌐rum⌐	Crab	E9	2	11
CVn	Canes Venatici	Canum Venatico-	Hunting Dogs	N12	11	5
CMa	Canis Major	Canis Majoris	Big Dog	E6	4	18
CMi	Canis Minor	Canis Minoris	Little Dog	E9	-	3
Cap	Capricornus	Capricorni	Sea Goat	E22	1	12
Car	Carina	Carinae	Keel	S9 (S3)	7	20
Cas	Cassiopeia	Cassiopeiae	(myth. name)	N2	8	17
Cen	Centaurus	Centauri	Centaur	S15 (S12)	4	26
Cep	Cepheus	Cephei	(myth. name)	N22	3	13
Cet	Cetus	Ceti	Whale	E0	2	18
Cha	Chamaeleon	Chamaeleontis	Chameleon	S9	-	4
Cir	Circinus	Circini	Compasses	S15	-	4
Col	Columba	Columbae	Dove	E2 (S3)	1	6
Com	Coma Berenices	Comae Berenices	Berenice's Hair	E13	13	8
CrA	Corona Australis	Coronae Australis	Southern Crown	S21	1	7
CrB	Corona Borealis	Coronae Borealis	Northern Crown	E15	-	10
Crv	Corvus	Corvi	Crow	E12	1	5
Crt	Crater	Crateris	Cup	E12	-	4
Cru	Crux	Crucis	Southern Cross	S12	2	7
Cyg	Cygnus	Cygni	Swan	N20 (N18)	8	31
Del	Delphinus	Delphini	Dolphin	E21	-	5
Dor	Dorado	Doradus	Dorado	S3	2	3
Dra	Draco	Draconis	Dragon	N16	4	21
Equ	Equuleus	Equulei	Little Horse	E23	-	4
Eri	Eridanus	Eridani	River	E2 (S0)	2	27
For	Fornax	Fornacis	Furnace	E2	3	3
Gem	Gemini	Geminorum	Twins	E7	3	17
Gru	Grus	Gruis	Crane (bird)	S24	-	8
Her	Hercules	Herculis	(myth. name)	N14 (E19)	3	23
Hor	Horologium	Horologii	Clock	S3 (S0)	-	2
Hya	Hydra	Hydrae	Water Snake	E10 (E12)	4	24
Hyi	Hydrus	Hydri	Little Water	S0	-	3
Ind	Indus	Indi	Indian ⌐Snake⌐	S24	-	3
Lac	Lacerta	Lacertae	Lizard	N24	2	7
Leo	Leo	Leonis	Lion	E11	8	17
LMi	Leo Minor	Leonis Minoris	Little Lion	N8	-	2

Abbr.	Constellation	Genitive	Meaning	Chart	Neb.	St.
Lep	Lepus	Leporis	Hare	E4	1	11
Lib	Libra	Librae	Balance (Scales)	E16	-	8
Lup	Lupus	Lupi	Wolf	S18	2	15
Lyn	Lynx	Lyncis	Lynx	N8 (N6)	1	8
Lyr	Lyra	Lyrae	Lyre	N18	2	8
Men	Mensa	Mensae	Table Mountain	S9	-	-
Mic	Microscopium	Microscopii	Microscope	E22	-	-
Mon	Monoceros	Monocerotis	Unicorn	E8 (E9)	7	9
Mus	Musca	Muscae	Fly	S12	-	6
Nor	Norma	Normae	Square	S18	2	2
Oct	Octans	Octantis	Octant	S24	-	3
Oph	Ophiuchus	Ophiuchi	Serpent-bearer	E17	11	21
Ori	Orion	Orionis	Hunter	E5 (E4)	8	24
Pav	Pavo	Pavonis	Peacock	S24	1	8
Peg	Pegasus	Pegasi	Winged Horse	E23	2	16
Per	Perseus	Persei	(myth. name)	N4	8	19
Phe	Phoenix	Phoenicis	Phoenix	S0	-	7
Pic	Pictor	Pictoris	Painter	S3	-	4
Psc	Pisces	Piscium	Fish (two)	E1 (E23)	1	19
PsA	Piscis Austrinus	Piscis Austrini	Southern Fish	E22	-	6
Pup	Puppis	Puppis	Stern	S6 (E6)	9	18
Pyx	Pyxis	Pyxidis	Compass	E10	-	3
Ret	Reticulum	Reticuli	Reticle	S3	-	4
Sge	Sagitta	Sagittae	Arrow	E21	1	5
Sgr	Sagittarius	Sagittarii	Archer	E20	18	16
Sco	Scorpius	Scorpii	Scorpion	E18 (S21)	7	22
Scl	Sculptor	Sculptoris	Sculptor	E0	3	3
Sct	Scutum	Scuti	Shield	E19	3	3
Ser	Serpens (Caput)	Serpentis (Caputis)	Serpent (Head)	E16	1	8
	(Cauda)	(Caudae)	(Tail)	E19	2	4
Sex	Sextans	Sextantis	Sextant	E10	1	3
Tau	Taurus	Tauri	Bull	E3	4	24
Tel	Telescopium	Telescopii	Telescope	S21	-	2
Tri	Triangulum	Trianguli	Triangle	N0	1	6
TrA	Triangulum Au-	Trianguli Australis	Southern Triangle	S24	-	5
Tuc	Tucana ⌊strale⌋	Tucanae	Toucan	S0 (S24)	3	3
UMa	Ursa Major	Ursae Majoris	Great Bear	N10 (N8)	11	24
UMi	Ursa Minor	Ursae Minoris	Little Bear	NP	-	8
Vel	Vela	Velorum	Sails	S6	4	16
Vir	Virgo	Virginis	Maiden	E16	17	13
Vol	Volans	Volantis	Flying Fish	S3	-	6
Vul	Vulpecula	Vulpeculae	Fox	E21	2	3
88	88 (89)	88 (89)	88 (89)	48	250	900

Chart: chart number(s) for the main part of the constellation
Neb., St.: number of nebulae and stars in the catalog

Key to the Star Charts

These four star charts indicate the way the celestial sphere is divided into the 48 charts on pp. 24–119. Most of the area is covered on the facing page, while polar regions are shown on this page. Solar positions are marked on the ecliptic (yellow). The charts' limiting magnitude is 4ᵐ5, their scale in declination is 14°/cm (≈ 36°/inch).

-1ᵐ   0ᵐ   1ᵐ   2ᵐ   3ᵐ   4ᵐ

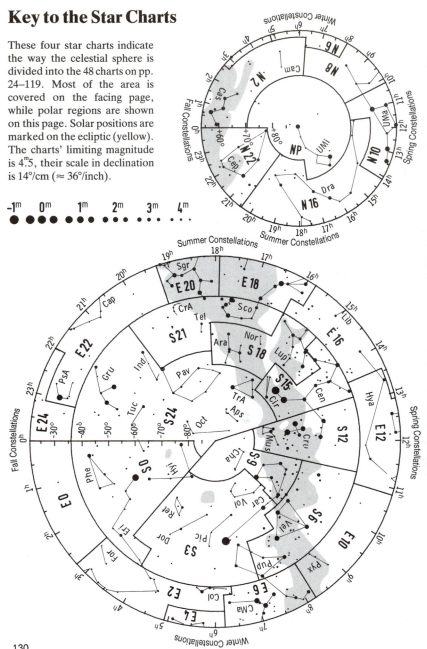